NIKOLAI ERDMAN

Born in Moscow in 1900, Erdman served briefly in the Red Army during the Civil War, before plunging into the bohemian life of post-Revolutionary Moscow, writing poetry and revue sketches. He associated with the Imaginist group between 1919 and 1924, and wrote sketches for the opening of the Moscow Theatre of Satire in 1924. Fame came with Meyerhold's production of Erdman's first play, *The Mandate,* in 1925, which was to be followed in 1928 by *The Suicide,* until it was banned by Stalin's censor in 1932 while in rehearsal at both Meyerhold's company and the Moscow Arts Theatre. Erdman's career suffered further setback when he was exiled from Moscow to Siberia for three years. On his return in the late 1930s he worked chiefly on filmscripts and libretti for operettas. Nadezhda Mandelstam writes of him at this time: 'Erdman himself chose to fall silent – anything just to stay alive . . . Very occasionally he would . . . tell me the plot of a play he had just thought of but would never write . . . ' His stage adaptation of Lermontov, *A Hero of our Time,* was staged in Moscow in 1965 by Yuri Lyubimov, who also co-wrote it. *The Suicide* was finally staged – but outside the USSR – in 1969, the year before Erdman's death in 1970.

DECLAN DONNELLAN

Declan Donnellan was born in England of Irish parents, grew up in London and was called to the Bar at the Middle Temple. With his partner, Nick Ormerod, he formed Cheek By Jowl in 1981. The company introduced British audiences to such European classics as Racine's *Andromache* (1985), Corneille's *The Cid* (1986), Ostrovsky's *A Family Affair* (1988) and Lessing's *Miss Sara Sampson* (1989). Internationally, the company is best known for its eleven productions of Shakespeare including *As You Like It* (1994), *Much Ado About Nothing* (1998) and *Othello* (2004). He is Associate Director of the National Theatre in London, where his productions include *Fuente Ovejuna* by Lope de Vega (1990), *Sweeney Todd* by Stephen Sondheim (1993), both parts of *Angels in America* by Tony Kushner (1991 and 1994) and *The Mandate* by Nikolai Erdman (2004). For the Royal Shakespeare Company, he directed *The School for Scandal* (1998) and inaugurated their Academy in 2002 with *King Lear*. For the Avignon Festival, he directed *Le Cid* (1998) and *The Winter's Tale* for the Maly Drama Theatre in St Petersburg (1997). Operas include Verdi's *Falstaff* with Claudio Abbado for the Salzburg Festival (2002) and he directed the ballet of *Romeo and Juliet* by Prokofiev for the Bolshoi (2003). Also in Moscow, he has formed a company of actors whose productions include *Boris Godunov* by Pushkin, *Twelfth Night*, and *Three Sisters* by Chekhov. His other translations include *Antigone* by Sophocles and *Don't Fool With Love* by Alfred de Musset. His book *The Actor and the Target* first appeared in Russian and has subsequently been published in French and in English. He has received several awards in Moscow, Paris, New York and London, including the Olivier for Outstanding Achievement. He is a Chevalier des Arts et des Lettres.

NIKOLAI ERDMAN

The Mandate

in an English Version by
DECLAN DONNELLAN

NICK HERN BOOKS
London

www.nickhernbooks.co.uk

A Nick Hern Book

The Mandate first published in Great Britain as a paperback original in 2004 by Nick Hern Books Limited, 14 Larden Road, London W3 7ST

Mandat copyright © the Estate of Nikolai Erdman

This translation of *The Mandate* copyright © 2004 Declan Donnellan

Introduction copyright © 2004 John Freedman

The Estate of Nikolai Erdman and Declan Donnellan have asserted their right to be identified as the authors of this work

Cover image: Getty Images, designed by Michael Mayhew

Typeset by Country Setting, Kingsdown, Kent CT14 8ES
Printed and bound in Great Britain by Bookmarque, Croydon, Surrey

A CIP catalogue record for this book is available from the British Library

ISBN 1 85459 825 2

Contents

Introduction

Nikolai Erdman's *The Mandate* is a comedy whose time has
come . . . again.

For the longest time, some 75 years in fact, it has existed to
one degree or another in the shadow of what is universally
considered to be Erdman's masterpiece, *The Suicide*. Like *The
Suicide*, *The Mandate* has experienced abrupt ups and downs
over the decades, debuting in 1925 as one of the most legendary
productions of the great director Vsevolod Meyerhold, completely disappearing from the radar screen between the 1930s
and the 1950s, being rediscovered with fanfare in Europe in
the 1970s and then settling into that awkward category of
'great and famous' plays that are seldom produced and even
less frequently produced well.

It is a curious state of affairs, actually, and we are fortunate
that Declan Donnellan has come along to accept the challenge
of a major revival. Donnellan has a special affinity for Russian
theatre, having worked in Russia frequently for the better part
of a decade. Moreover, he is commendably free of prejudice
in his judgments. When confronted with the oft-repeated
opinion that *The Mandate* is somehow a second-rate legend
in comparison to *The Suicide*, he blithely replied, 'Strange.
It's always been self-evident to me that *The Mandate* is every
bit *The Suicide's* equal.' Time will tell, of course, but the
version Donnellan has created for his production at the
National Theatre may well be the one that finally brings this
side-splitting, thought-provoking and sometimes chilling
comedy home to us.

Erdman himself, who was born in Moscow at the dawn of a
new century in 1900 and died virtually unknown outside of
professional circles at the age of 69 in 1970, is one of the most
elusive figures in the history of Russian theatre and cinema.
From the mid-1920s to the early 1930s he was, for all intents
and purposes, the in-house playwright for Meyerhold; he was

respected as a writer of unrivalled talent by the great filmmaker Sergei Eisenstein; and over the decades he acquired the reputation as the Soviet Union's most reliable script doctor, often working without credit: he co-scripted two of the Soviet Union's most beloved musical comedies, *Jolly Fellows* (1934) and *Volga-Volga* (1938), the latter of which was known to be Joseph Stalin's favourite film. The great poet and playwright Vladimir Mayakovsky once said simply to Erdman, 'Nikolai Robertovich, teach me how to write a play!' And in 1964, when Yury Lyubimov founded the soon-to-be world-famous Taganka Theatre in Moscow, he enlisted his old friend Nikolai Erdman to be a trusted advisor, in part because of Erdman's direct links to Meyerhold and in part because of Erdman's unsurpassed instincts for theatre.

Yet precious little has reached us from this writer whom Meyerhold compared in stature to Nikolai Gogol, and whose play *The Suicide* Konstantin Stanislavsky called 'a work of genius'. The chaos of history and Erdman's own self-effacing personality conspired to make this so.

The Russians often quote a Chinese proverb that cautions, 'God forbid you should live in interesting times.' Erdman came of age in one of the most, shall we say, *fascinating* eras in all of modern history. He was 17 when the Bolsheviks deposed Tsar Nicholas II in 1917. When he was a 19-year-old recruit serving in the Red Army during the Russian Civil War, his first highly-crafted poems were published. As Vladimir Lenin's New Economic Policy was being put in place to revive the moribund Soviet economy in 1922, Erdman began writing his first comic sketches and parodies for the burgeoning nightclub and music hall scene in Moscow. *The Mandate*, his first full-length play, was one of the inaugural works to be staged at the new Vsevolod Meyerhold Theatre in 1925.

The Suicide, his next major play, the original draft of which was completed in 1928, became one of the first casualties of the advancing Stalinist age. This tragi-farce about a simple man who is nearly pushed to suicide by a horde of unscrupulous people wishing to exploit his despair for their own purposes, caused a firestorm of reactions at a time when art and literature were key components in the evolving political life of the country. Backed by such luminaries as Meyerhold and Stanislavsky, both of whom planned to stage *The Suicide* at their theatres, and attacked fiercely by legions of aggressive cultural bureaucrats and narrow-minded writers loyal to the dogma of the Communist Party, the play fell into limbo – famous throughout Russia because of the hot public debate surrounding it, but neither published nor staged. When it was banned for the third and final time in 1932, Erdman barely had another year left before his life would be altered irreversibly. Combining work and play in the autumn of 1933, he was present in the Black Sea resort town of Gagry for the filming of *Jolly Fellows*. There, according to an eyewitness, 'At the height of an October seaside day, they arrested the fragile, utterly charming Erdman and carried him away like they carry away furniture.'

In short biographies, the next phrase usually reads: 'Erdman never wrote another play.' And this is true, although, perhaps, misleading. While still in exile – he spent three years living in 'free confinement' in the Siberian cities of Yeniseisk (1933-34) and then Tomsk (1934-36) – he began and then abandoned a play that was never finished. He never did start another. This aborted play, *The Hypnotist*, was intended to tell the satiric tale of a stranger causing bedlam in a town by telling its residents the truths none of them wished to know. Apparently having realised that such a play at that time was unthinkable, perhaps even suicidal, Erdman sensed he had reached the end of the line as a dramatist.

Life, of course, is messier and more complex than the constraints of potted biography would allow. The fact is that Erdman continued to write, one might even say prolifically. The list of popular films created from his scripts between 1938 and 1970 is long indeed. Several generations of young Russians have grown up on the wise and witty characters he created in timeless animated films and cinematic fairy tales. Moreover, several of those films feature sensitive artists or intellectuals engaged in the eternal struggle with stupid despots. But that was in cinema, a sphere in which the screenwriter is far more invisible than the playwright in theatre. Barring some comic interludes inserted into other

writers' works and a few dramatisations of classic novels, Erdman never wrote for the theatre again. It is another thing that the annals of Russian drama are filled with writers who left behind only a handful of plays, but whose influence has been lasting. This puts Erdman right in the middle of a rich tradition.

Meyerhold's production of *The Mandate* was greeted with unprecedented enthusiasm by the critics and enjoyed tremendous popularity with audiences. By the following season it was being performed in over forty theatres throughout Russia. It was said to be the first play to reflect recognisable Soviet characters and problems while it was hailed as the first Soviet play successfully to incorporate the lessons of the masters in a modern context. Indeed, it comprised a mélange of styles that included the 19th-century European vaudeville, traditional Russian 'serious comedy', the slapstick of cabaret humour and the grotesquerie of the tragicomic farce. Erdman was compared repeatedly to Gogol and Alexander Sukhovo-Kobylin, the 19th-century author of a trilogy of devastating black satires about the dark side of Russian life. For good measure, Erdman was also compared to Anton Chekhov for the lyrical qualities of his characters and to the great bard of Russian merchant mores, Alexander Ostrovsky. It was from Ostrovsky that, in altered form, Erdman borrowed the social setting of *The Mandate*, the household of a déclassé merchant family, and the personality types of two central characters, an overbearing mother Nadejda Petrovna and her spoiled, irascible son Pavel Guliachkin.

It is easy to overlook, however, how quickly things were changing in the Soviet Union in the 1920s. By 1927, even as *The Mandate* was achieving its first international recognition with a production at the Renaissance Theatre in Berlin, Soviet critics were beginning to snip and peck at the play, accusing it of being out-of-step with the new Soviet reality. By the early '30s, the censors had taken aim at it, repeatedly insisting that more and more lines be cut from performances. By the time Erdman was arrested in 1933, the sole remaining production of the play in the Soviet Union – Meyerhold's – was performed for the final time. Only after Stalin's death in 1953 could there be any thought of someone coming back to the play. But even then, the few attempts were to no avail. A handsome book version was prepared for publication, but it was cancelled before going beyond the mock-up stage. In fact, in a ghostly echo of the way the play had disappeared so completely, the designer's mock-up had everything in place – the page decorations, the illustrations, the page numbers, the title, the act and scene markers – but the spaces on the page for the actual dialogue were eloquently left blank. Erast Garin, the legendary actor who performed as Guliachkin for Meyerhold, mounted a revival in Moscow in 1956 but this show closed soon after it opened. And that was the end of the story until the celebrated world premiere of *The Suicide* in Gothenburg, Sweden, in 1969. Erdman lived to hear tell of the resurrection of *The Suicide*, but by the time *The Mandate* returned to the boards in Germany in 1971, he had been dead for ten months.

Unlike *The Suicide*, which enjoyed enormous success at the Royal Shakespeare Company in 1979 and 1980 and was an international hit throughout the 1970s and '80s (even being translated into Flemish and Afrikaans), *The Mandate* has, until now, never quite taken hold in English. The best it did in Britain and North America was a small production here and a radio broadcast there (Peter Tegel's translation for BBC Radio 3 in 1976).

This might well change with Donnellan's fresh approach to it. His is a sharp, breezy, conversational rendition that skips forward easily and clearly. In doing so, he has captured the essence of Erdman's style, which is renowned for its effervescent strings of composite puns and witty wisecracks that go off like chains of firecrackers. Famously, one scholar counted 336 bursts of laughter at a performance of *The Mandate* at Meyerhold's theatre in 1926. Cleaving to Polonius's observation that brevity is the soul of wit, Donnellan has fashioned a text of pithy exchanges that propel the plot, the characters' thoughts and their frequent hilarious asides forward at a brisk speed. This is the Erdman trademark, rolling and crackling, multiple layers of humour that feed on one another and egg each other on as they develop.

The storyline is at once riotously convoluted and classically simple. The ingredients include mistaken identities, witting and unwitting impostors, three weddings arranged among three people in the course of two days, a little bit of harmless political subterfuge and a lot of slapstick comedy – including a man stubbornly wearing an overturned pot of noodles on his head and a cook being taken for an Imperial Princess when she hides under a rug. The moving forces in the play are two disparate and desperate families – the impoverished Guliachkins and the wealthy Smetaniches – who come together on a collision course as each tries to survive in the new Soviet republic.

But Erdman would not be Erdman, and Russian drama would not be what it is, if this were merely a goofball comedy about social hangers-on. In fact, woven into all of the tomfoolery are the kinds of provocative and disturbing themes that make up the meat and potatoes of the Russian literary tradition.

The Mandate is populated by individuals who have been cast adrift. The collapse of one social structure (in this case, Tsarist Russia) and the rapid rise of one that is vastly different (in this case, a proletarian state) have made outcasts of the once-comfortable Guliachkins and Smetaniches. Each and every one has been stripped of the identity with which they always have defined themselves. So, on one level, *The Mandate* is a play about people struggling to recreate themselves in alien and hostile circumstances. That they do it badly, clumsily and stupidly is an obvious sign we are dealing with a knockabout comedy. Backed into a corner and under attack, Pavel Guliachkin, unexpectedly even for himself, flails in his mind for the most threatening word he can imagine and blurts out that he is a Communist. Then, warming up to the role of an impostor, he even takes up a briefcase to provide material proof of his importance and punctuates that by writing out a mandate that he does, in fact, live where he lives. Olymp Smetanich decides to marry off his son, first to the sister of this 'Communist Party member' when that seems an expedient way to ingratiate himself with the powers that be and next, when he believes the political winds have changed, to a woman he takes for the only surviving daughter of the assassinated Nicholas II.

On the surface these are silly people doing even sillier things. But this does not alter the essence of the problem, its gravity and its tragic consequences. These are people whose sense of self has been wiped out utterly by a faceless and momentous social upheaval. Stripped of the reality which has given them shape and substance as individuals, they frantically seek, through the power of imagination and the instinct of panic, to establish new ones into which, perhaps, they may be able to fit. Nothing is what it seems, however, and they cannot recover solid ground regardless of what they do. Pavel's mandate is no mandate at all. And if Pavel is no Communist and Nastia no princess, then what is the point of Smetanich arranging a match for his son with either Pavel's sister or Nastia? Obviously, none. It all is a dream, as Calderòn might have said, and an empty and misleading one at that.

Erdman came into being as a writer at a time when the power, and thus the danger, of words were beginning to be felt with new force. It was the dawn of an age in which mass culture – something that seems as natural as the air we breathe now – was in its infancy. This included the proliferation of populist newspapers, pulp fiction, the mesmerising images of cinema, the miracle of recorded music that could be played back on a phonograph, and a political climate in which leaders, through seductive, accessible slogans for the first time appeared – I emphasise, *appeared* – to be appealing to common people for support. This created a massive, yet subtle, mind-altering assault on humanity. One strongly suspects that the pressures of those changes were similar to what we are experiencing in the 21st century when leapfrogging advances in technology transform our universe beyond recognition overnight; when through shrewd promotional tactics corporations foist their agendas upon us under the guise of advances in fashion and opportunity; when politicians through soundbites devised by virtuoso spin doctors assure us that black is white; and journalists, either intimidated or incriminated, write and report the stories that make this status quo seem not only legitimate, not only inevitable but desirable. In Erdman's world, as in ours, individuals increasingly were finding themselves at the mercy of a relentless barrage of words, signs and symbols, almost all of which were flawed if not downright false.

Witness the cook Nastia, so immersed in her romantic novel that she isn't always able to differentiate between a man who has sneaked up behind her and the dashing fictional character she is reading about. As she keeps slipping back into fantasy, she admits it's just an 'automatic' mistake. Consider Pavel's mother assuring her son that if he joins the ruling party, he will get to ride around in a motor car. He doesn't think much of the former idea, but the latter is too enticing to turn down. Incidents of this sort are myriad in *The Mandate*; characters are constantly finding themselves influenced by catchphrases and clichés and they invariably alter their behaviour willingly as a result. Words, whether purposefully fallacious or merely erroneously understood, exert an ominous effect on their lives. Some characters, perhaps like some of us in our age, simply have begun to tune it all out – Pavel's mother admits she doesn't know what a picture is for because she doesn't read the newspapers, while her daughter Varvara blithely confides she was paying no attention when the regime began crippling art. Victims that they are, in other words, these are people who allow themselves to become pawns in others' games.

These failings of character and judgment, of course, are what set up the play's potential for revelation and raise its problems to the level of philosophy and ethics. Pavel Guliachkin, the impostor, the self-proclaimed commissar, so grows into his imagined persona that he begins manifesting an alarming proclivity for fascist behaviour. His journey becomes the prototypical nightmare of a little man tasting far too much power. But rather than stop it there, Erdman throws another twist into the works – as soon as Pavel reaches the apex of his self-induced delusion, he is sent crashing down again, exposed as a petty, even unimaginative, faker. Like everyone in the play, he is left pondering the ultimate question: how can he live now knowing what he does?

Erdman in *The Mandate* is not so much asking the traditional Russian questions of 'what is to be done?' or 'who is to blame?' as he is introducing a question that perhaps suits our own age better than any other: 'What has occurred here and how could it possibly have happened?' *The Mandate* is a play that, while entertaining us royally, will not let us off the hook.

It is a play that encapsulates problems and forces that are as prevalent today as when it was written 80 years ago. And finally, despite having spent so many decades in relative eclipse, this play emerges as the masterful work of an author who in sensibility, outlook and understanding, remains very much our contemporary.

John Freedman

John Freedman is theatre critic of *The Moscow Times* and author of *Silence's Roar: The Life and Drama of Nikolai Erdman.*

This version of *The Mandate* was first performed in the
Cottesloe auditorium of the National Theatre, London, on
26 October 2004, with the following cast:

Pavel Sergeevich Guliachkin	Martin Hutson
Nadejda Petrovna Guliachkina	Deborah Findlay
Ivan Ivanovich Shironkin	Adrian Scarborough
Varvara Sergeevna Guliachkina	Naomi Frederick
Anastasia Nikolaevna (Nastia)	Sinead Matthews
Tamara Leopoldovna	Carol Macready
Organ-grinder	Roger Sloman
Olymp Valerianovich Smetanich	Bruce Alexander
Valerian Olympovich	Laurence Penry-Jones
Woman with a parrot and a tambourine	Anne White
Man with a drum	Sean Jackson
Autonom Sygizmundovich	David Collings
Agaphangel	Harry Towb
Anatoly	Daniel Hart
Feliziata Gordeevna	Anne White
Ilyinkin	Sean Jackson
Ilyinkina	Carol Macready
Zarkhin	Roger Sloman
Ariadna Pavlinovna Zarkhina	Sarah-Jane Drummey
Krantic Narkis Smaragdovich	Michael Rouse

Other parts played by members of the company.

Director   Declan Donnellan
Designer   Nick Ormerod
Director of Movement   Jane Gibson
Lighting Designer   Judith Greenwood
Music   Catherine Jayes
Sound Designer   Rich Walsh

THE MANDATE

Characters

PAVEL SERGEEVICH GULIACHKIN, *a young man*
NADEJDA PETROVNA GULIACHKINA, *his mother*
VARVARA SERGEEVNA GULIACHKINA, *his sister*
IVAN IVANOVICH SHIRONKIN, *their lodger*

NASTIA (ANASTASIA NIKOLAEVNA), *the Guliachkins' cook*
TAMARA LEOPOLDOVNA, *a friend of Nadejda's*

OLYMP VALERIANOVICH SMETANICH
VALERIAN, *his elder son*
ANATOLY, *his younger son*
AUTONOM SYGIZMUNDOVICH
AGAPHANGEL, *a servant, ex-soldier*

STEPAN STEPANOVICH
FELIZIATA GORDEEVNA, *his wife*
ILYINKIN
ILYINKINA, *his wife*
ZARKHIN
ARIADNA PAVLINOVNA ZARKHINA, *his wife*
TOSIA, *their daughter*
SIUSIA, *their daughter*
KRANTIC NARKIS SMARAGDOVICH

AN ORGAN-GRINDER
A MAN *with a drum*
A WOMAN *with a parrot and a tambourine*
A CARETAKER
A TAXI-DRIVER / PORTERS (*non-speaking*)

ACT ONE

The GULIACHKINS' *flat.*

PAVEL SERGEEVICH GULIACHKIN *is standing on a stepladder, hanging pictures, watched by his mother,* NADEJDA PETROVNA. *On the floor are pictures in frames.*

PAVEL SERGEEVICH. Now, Mummy, just hand me 'Copenhagen Twilight'.

NADEJDA PETROVNA. No, Pavel dear, 'In Thee, Oh Lord, I Trust' would go much better.

PAVEL SERGEEVICH. No, Mummy. 'Copenhagen Twilight' will look much more artistic.

NADEJDA PETROVNA. Well, whatever you think best, Pavel dear, but I've always wanted to hang 'In Thee, Oh Lord, I Trust' there in the middle. It's got a more showy frame, Pavel dear, and its content is deeper than 'Copenhagen Twilight'.

PAVEL SERGEEVICH. If it's content you're after, Mummy, just take a look at it. Now take a look at the other side.

NADEJDA PETROVNA (*looking at the other side of the picture*). How perfectly ghastly! Who on earth is that?

PAVEL SERGEEVICH. There's no point in being disgusted, Mummy, times have changed.

NADEJDA PETROVNA. But whoever is it, Pavel dear?

PAVEL SERGEEVICH. That's his name underneath, Mummy.

NADEJDA PETROVNA. I thought so! I knew it was a foreigner! (*On the other side is a picture of Karl Marx.*) What exactly made you choose this one, Pavel dear? 'Copenhagen Twilight' has been hanging here for a good eighteen years – a pleasure to the eye and inoffensive to all guests.

PAVEL SERGEEVICH. Really, Mummy, sometimes you behave like a complete unconscious social element. Tell me, what do you think a picture is *for*?

NADEJDA PETROVNA. However should I know, Pavel dear? I don't read newspapers.

PAVEL SERGEEVICH. Nevertheless, Mummy: what, do you suppose, exactly, a picture *is*?

NADEJDA PETROVNA. Well, I remember years ago, in the old days, Pavel dear, a clerk from the post office used to have his dinner with us, and he always used to say: 'You should know,' he used to say, 'Nadejda Petrovna, a painting is no less than the soul's deep moan when pleasured by the organ of sight.'

PAVEL SERGEEVICH. That may have been true once, but nowadays a picture must be a weapon of propaganda.

NADEJDA PETROVNA. A weapon? However's that!?

PAVEL SERGEEVICH. I shall explain. For example, say an official calls round one day and sees 'In Thee, Oh Lord, I Trust' hanging on the wall, he'll get suspicious: 'Tell me,' he'll ask, 'Citizen Guliachkin, what did your grandfather do?'

NADEJDA PETROVNA. He didn't do anything, he just had a business.

PAVEL SERGEEVICH. And precisely what kind of business was it?

NADEJDA PETROVNA. A laundry business.

PAVEL SERGEEVICH. What?

NADEJDA PETROVNA. He had a laundry, I'd say.

PAVEL SERGEEVICH. A laundry, indeed? Perhaps I should take you to court for such bourgeois superstitions?

NADEJDA PETROVNA. Good Heavens!

PAVEL SERGEEVICH. Heavens or no Heavens, that's how things are now.

NADEJDA PETROVNA. How can honest people live these days?

PAVEL SERGEEVICH. We have to manoeuvre, Mummy, we have to manoeuvre. Even though I never got through the Academy, I can still see right through their little revolution.

NADEJDA PETROVNA. But it's all so complicated, Pavel dear, how can you see right through it?

PAVEL SERGEEVICH. That's simple, I look through a hole, Mummy, through a hole.

NADEJDA PETROVNA. Through a hole? Through which hole, Pavel dear?

PAVEL SERGEEVICH. As you know, Mummy, we have a frosted glass door in the hallway. I've bored a hole in it.

NADEJDA PETROVNA. Good Heavens, whatever for?

PAVEL SERGEEVICH. I'll tell you what for. Say somebody rings the bell. You look through the hole – and you see who is ringing the bell and what he wants. Say, for example, it's the head of the housing committee, or even worse – a commissar from the Militia.

NADEJDA PETROVNA. Oh, God forbid!

PAVEL SERGEEVICH. Not at all. The moment you see a visitor like this through the hole, Mummy, you turn the picture over immediately – and bring him right into the sitting room as cool as a cucumber.

NADEJDA PETROVNA. And what then?

PAVEL SERGEEVICH. Well, then the commissar just hangs around for a bit, spots the picture, and then off he goes.

NADEJDA PETROVNA. Why would he do that, Pavel dear?

PAVEL SERGEEVICH. Because for them, Karl Marx is top boss.

NADEJDA PETROVNA. You've worked it all out so cleverly, but that Mr Marx will spoil my cosy ambience.

PAVEL SERGEEVICH. Not at all, Mummy. If it's someone you know, you can leave it as 'Copenhagen Twilight' – (*He turns the picture back.*) – so even if someone like Smetanich were to drop in, he'd think we were intellectuals and not revolutionaries.

NADEJDA PETROVNA. You know, Pavel dear, Smetanich did promise to call on us today.

PAVEL SERGEEVICH. What do you mean, promised to call on us?

NADEJDA PETROVNA. Just like this, he said, 'I'll drop round and take a look at your son and get an idea of how you live.'

PAVEL SERGEEVICH. Why on earth didn't you say so before, Mummy? This is extraordinary! Quick! Hang up 'In Thee, Oh Lord, I Trust'. Did he, Mummy, use those precise words: 'to take a look at your son'?

NADEJDA PETROVNA. Those words exactly.

PAVEL SERGEEVICH. I'll put on my new trousers.

NADEJDA PETROVNA. Wait, there's something I haven't told you! Smetanich wants to marry his son to our dear Varvara.

PAVEL SERGEEVICH. Marry?

NADEJDA PETROVNA. Yes.

PAVEL SERGEEVICH. Marry his son to our Varvara?

NADEJDA PETROVNA. Yes.

PAVEL SERGEEVICH. Excuse me, Mummy, but are you having one of your funny turns?

NADEJDA PETROVNA. No, Pavel dear, the Good Lord has been merciful today.

PAVEL SERGEEVICH. But how can he want to marry his son to our Varvara, when he's never even seen our Varvara?

NADEJDA PETROVNA. Is that so very important?

PAVEL SERGEEVICH. I'm not sure. Perhaps it's just as well he's never actually seen her. Are you quite sure this is true?

NADEJDA PETROVNA. Would I lie to my own son?

PAVEL SERGEEVICH. So, Mummy, soon we'll be relatives of Smetanich? – He's loaded!

NADEJDA PETROVNA. I wouldn't be too sure. The dowry is going to be a problem.

PAVEL SERGEEVICH. Dowry? Then forget it. You know perfectly well we haven't a bean.

NADEJDA PETROVNA. Oh, he doesn't need money, Pavel dear.

PAVEL SERGEEVICH. So how does he want the dowry paid, Mummy?

NADEJDA PETROVNA. In livestock, dear.

PAVEL SERGEEVICH. What do you mean, in livestock?

NADEJDA PETROVNA. Pavel dear, as Varvara's dowry he's asking for a . . . a Communist.

PAVEL SERGEEVICH. What? A Communist?

NADEJDA PETROVNA. Exactly.

PAVEL SERGEEVICH. Is it legal to trade in Party members, Mummy?

NADEJDA PETROVNA. If you just pick one up off the street, then of course it's illegal! But if he's your own, one you already happen to have at home, so to speak, then it's perfectly legal.

PAVEL SERGEEVICH. Mummy, we're Orthodox! We don't have any Communists!

NADEJDA PETROVNA. Fear not, my little lamb. I'm going to say a prayer and God will forgive our little sin.

PAVEL SERGEEVICH. What little sin?

NADEJDA PETROVNA. You'll have to join the Party, my pet.

PAVEL SERGEEVICH. Me? Join the Party?

NADEJDA PETROVNA. Yes, lambkin, you, my darling Pasha. Smetanich is depending on you.

PAVEL SERGEEVICH. Could you hold me steady, Mummy, it's all gone a bit dark.

NADEJDA PETROVNA. Just think about it, Pashikins dear: we'll marry our dear Varvara off, I'll go to live in Smetanich's luxurious flat, my grandsons will be born educated . . .

PAVEL SERGEEVICH. And me, Mummy, what will I do?

NADEJDA PETROVNA. Whatever you like: do officials ever have anything to do? You'll be driven round in a motor car, can you imagine it! Pavel my sweet, you'll go round in a motor car, and I'll pray for you to our Blessed Saviour. You'll drive round and round, and I'll pray, you going round and round and me praying away, what a life we'll have!

PAVEL SERGEEVICH. Driving round and round? All right, Mummy, I'll think about it.

NADEJDA PETROVNA. Think about it, Pavel dear, do think about it. And another thing . . .

PAVEL SERGEEVICH. Don't interrupt me, Mummy, I'm thinking. Actually, Mummy, you know it would really rather suit me to be an official. The slightest irritation and I'd bang my fist down on the table – 'Be quiet!'

He hits his hammer on the wall, and a crash is heard offstage.

NADEJDA PETROVNA. Oh, Heavens, I think you've just knocked the lodger's dishes off the shelf!

IVAN IVANOVICH SHIRONKIN *rushes into the room. On his head is a cooking pot.*

IVAN IVANOVICH. Got you now! You'll pay for this, citizen. Don't think I'll leave it here! I'm reporting you to the authorities!

PAVEL SERGEEVICH. What right do you have to shout in a domestic residence?

IVAN IVANOVICH. What right?! You've drowned me in noodles!

PAVEL SERGEEVICH. If I may . . .

IVAN IVANOVICH. No you may not!

Enter PAVEL*'s sister,* VARVARA SERGEEVNA GULIACHKINA.

VARVARA SERGEEVNA. Whatever's going on?

NADEJDA PETROVNA. What is wrong, Ivan Ivanovich? Whatever's the matter with you?

IVAN IVANOVICH. How many times have I told you, Nadejda Petrovna, that my work requires calm and quiet, and yet you insist on banging nails into my wall?

NADEJDA PETROVNA. We don't go near your nails, Ivan Ivanovich, so please don't touch ours, after all, we are in our own room.

IVAN IVANOVICH. But pardon me, Nadejda Petrovna, I cook my meals myself . . .

NADEJDA PETROVNA. Yes, and that smell gets everywhere!

IVAN IVANOVICH. Excuse me, Nadejda Petrovna, I am a single man and do not have cohabiters, unlike certain other people I could mention. And if I use a kerosene burner, it's only because every human being has to eat.

NADEJDA PETROVNA. Please spare us your sleeping arrangements – my daughter is a virgin.

VARVARA SERGEEVNA. Oh, Mummy, don't exaggerate!

IVAN IVANOVICH. Spare you?! I was saving that pan of noodles on my top shelf, and you bang away and shove it on my head!

NADEJDA PETROVNA. We are not responsible for your noodles.

IVAN IVANOVICH. Oh, you're not responsible, are you? I suppose you could go on banging away on my wall till every pan crashes on top of me, till I'm drowned and suffocated by noodles . . . and you'd say you weren't responsible for that either!?

NADEJDA PETROVNA. People don't drown in noodles, Ivan Ivanovich, only cockroaches do.

IVAN IVANOVICH. The Militia will sort this out; I'm making an official complaint.

NADEJDA PETROVNA. Do you think, Ivan Ivanovich, that I'm some sort of female convict to be mentioned in official complaints?

VARVARA SERGEEVNA. You'd better take the pot off your head, Ivan Ivanovich, it's not a hat – it must be very uncomfortable.

IVAN IVANOVICH. Certainly not! I'm not stupid. You get me to take it off now and then where is my proof? Nice try! Ha! You must think I'm stupid! I shall go to Comrade Commissar just like this and explain: 'Here, Comrade Commissar, is concrete proof of a Disturbance of the Communal Peace.' Yes, indeed. For you – it's just a pot, but for us – it's forensic evidence.

NADEJDA PETROVNA. So are you going to walk down the street with your evidence on your head?

IVAN IVANOVICH. Just like this.

NADEJDA PETROVNA. They'll put you in a lunatic asylum.

IVAN IVANOVICH. There are no lunatic asylums any more. The People Are Free.

NADEJDA PETROVNA. Shout at him, would you, Pavel dear?

PAVEL SERGEEVICH. Shout at him? What good would that do, Mummy? He won't listen.

NADEJDA PETROVNA. Oh, do shout at him all the same, sweetheart, otherwise he might really go to the Militia.

IVAN IVANOVICH. Don't you whisper with your son, Nadejda Petrovna. I, Nadejda Petrovna, will not be intimidated by your son. I, Nadejda Petrovna, am afraid of nobody. For me, Nadejda Petrovna . . .

PAVEL SERGEEVICH. Silence! I am a member of the Party.

Everyone, including PAVEL SERGEEVICH, *is frightened.* IVAN IVANOVICH *walks backwards out of fright and leaves.*

Mummy, I'm leaving for the Caucasus.

NADEJDA PETROVNA. Why?

VARVARA SERGEEVNA. Whatever for?

PAVEL SERGEEVICH. They could shoot me for using words like that.

VARVARA SERGEEVNA. Shoot you?

NADEJDA PETROVNA. There's no such law, Pavel dear. They can't shoot you just for using words.

PAVEL SERGEEVICH. There are words and there are words, Mummy.

NADEJDA PETROVNA. I've heard all sorts of words during my married life, all kinds of words. In fact, the late Sergei Tarasovich managed to use words which are impossible to convey to an unmarried person. And even he died his own natural death of vodka, and you are telling me . . .

VARVARA SERGEEVNA. Please, Mummy, don't upset yourself, he's just talking nonsense.

PAVEL SERGEEVICH. Please try to understand, Mummy, that in point of fact, I am not nor have ever been a member of the Party.

NADEJDA PETROVNA. Then become one now, sign up.

PAVEL SERGEEVICH. I know. I could become one now and sign up.

NADEJDA PETROVNA. Well, thank Heavens! Finally! Varvara, we'll be able to have that wedding of yours after all. Now thank your brother for agreeing.

VARVARA SERGEEVNA. Merci.

PAVEL SERGEEVICH. But what if they won't accept me, Mummy?

NADEJDA PETROVNA. But, Pavel dear, they accept all sorts of riff-raff.

PAVEL SERGEEVICH. On this particular point, Mummy, do you happen to know Comrade Utkin?

NADEJDA PETROVNA. The one who fell out of the airplane?

PAVEL SERGEEVICH. That was Utochkin, Mummy; this is Comrade Utkin.

NADEJDA PETROVNA. No, I don't know him.

PAVEL SERGEEVICH. Well, I ran into him on the train to Samara when I went to get the bread. He looks a real yob, but in fact, three of his relatives are Communists. I think I'll invite them round and get them to recommend me to the Party.

NADEJDA PETROVNA. Oh yes, do invite them, Pavel dear, do, please.

PAVEL SERGEEVICH. And remember, Mummy, that if they find out we used to have a grocery shop, we'll really be in the soup.

NADEJDA PETROVNA. How would they find that out, Pavel dear? They couldn't.

PAVEL SERGEEVICH. I'm telling you this so you don't make any political boobs when they come round.

NADEJDA PETROVNA. Don't be silly, Pavel dear. I'll treat them to some home cooking. 'Dearest comrade,' I'll say. 'Go on, help yourself to another vol-au-vent.'

PAVEL SERGEEVICH. Have you gone completely insane, Mummy? Do you think Communists eat vol-au-vents? You might just as well give them crème brûlée! And as a matter of fact, Mummy, if I'm to be the sacrificial victim for the family, you'll all have to start doing what I say.

NADEJDA PETROVNA. Don't we, Pavel dear . . . ?

PAVEL SERGEEVICH. Silence! I'm telling you for the last time, Mummy: by the evening, every scrap of food in this flat must be of unadulterated proletarian origin, and no 'In Thee, Oh Lord, I Trust's. Have I made myself perfectly clear?

NADEJDA PETROVNA. Perfectly clear, Pavel dear.

PAVEL SERGEEVICH. And if Varvara blurts one word about God or the grocery shop, I swear to you I'll run away to the Caucasus.

VARVARA SERGEEVNA. But it's all so very peculiar . . .

PAVEL SERGEEVICH. Don't you try and 'but' me, Varvara. All because of you, a young man in the peak of health is being cannibalised into a human dowry, and you have the nerve to argue.

NADEJDA PETROVNA. Varvara dear, apologise immediately to your brother.

VARVARA SERGEEVNA. But, Mummy . . .

NADEJDA PETROVNA. Varvara!

VARVARA SERGEEVNA. But, Mummy . . .

NADEJDA PETROVNA. Don't be stubborn, Varvara!

VARVARA SERGEEVNA. I apologise.

PAVEL SERGEEVICH. All right, I'm off.

NADEJDA PETROVNA. Where to, Pavel dear? To Comrade Utkin?

PAVEL SERGEEVICH. To Comrade Utkin, Mummy, to Comrade Utkin. Dear God, I'm just about to ruin my life.

NADEJDA PETROVNA. What's wrong with you, Pavel dear?

PAVEL SERGEEVICH. How can I invite them here, Mummy, when we don't have a single relative from the working classes?

NADEJDA PETROVNA. For you, Pavel dear, I'd buy anything, but what I don't have – I don't have.

PAVEL SERGEEVICH. We'll just have to find some proletarians and pretend they're our relatives. Varvara dear, do you know any members of the working class?

VARVARA SERGEEVNA. You must be joking. I've never even spoken to a bank clerk.

PAVEL SERGEEVICH. Now what can I do, Mummy?

NADEJDA PETROVNA. Wait, let's ask our Nastia. Nastia! Nastia! Confound the girl, she must be reading some book again. Nastia!

PAVEL SERGEEVICH. Are you deaf, Varvara? Call Nastia, your mother is going hoarse.

VARVARA SERGEEVNA. My singing teacher has forbidden me to raise my voice, he's just discovered I'm a natural coloratura.

PAVEL SERGEEVICH. Well, then, die a virgin coloratura.

NADEJDA PETROVNA. Do you want to spoil everything, Varvara? Shout when you are told to!

VARVARA SERGEEVNA. Nastia!

PAVEL SERGEEVICH. What a truly horrible voice you have, Varvara, absolutely unbearable, I can't imagine . . .

VARVARA SERGEEVNA. Unbearable? My singing teacher told me . . .

PAVEL SERGEEVICH. Your singing teacher is a fool. Nastia!

EVERYONE. Nastia!

Enter ANASTASIA NIKOLAEVNA (NASTIA), *their cook.*

NASTIA. Here I am!

NADEJDA PETROVNA. What are you shouting for? Why are you screaming your head off? I'm asking you, where do you think you are – in a house or in the street?

NASTIA. I . . .

NADEJDA PETROVNA. Shut your mouth when I'm talking to you. You should have been born a sergeant-major, not a cook. Don't contradict me. Why don't you come when I call you? Have you been reading those books again? Tell me? Do I pay you wages so you can spend it on books? Tell me?

PAVEL SERGEEVICH. Mummy, calm yourself. I need to ask you, Nastia: do you ever receive visits from members of the working class?

NASTIA. Pavel Sergeevich, I'm not that kind of girl.

PAVEL SERGEEVICH. That's not what I'm talking about, Nastia. I'm asking you: do you have acquaintances from the working class?

NASTIA. I'm not that kind of girl; I don't have acquaintances.

NADEJDA PETROVNA. Nastia, you're a silly girl, don't lie!

NASTIA. I've had loads of different employers, and they'll all swear I've never had acquaintances. Go and ask any of them.

NADEJDA PETROVNA. Nastia, silly girl, don't tell lies, I'm warning you.

NASTIA. Oh well, Nadejda Petrovna, if you mean Ivan
  Ivanovich, but he's not an acquaintance, he's a lodger.

NADEJDA PETROVNA. What?

NASTIA. And when he invited me to his room it was only
  because he wanted to enlarge my bust.

VARVARA SERGEEVNA. What?

PAVEL SERGEEVICH. What for?

NASTIA. Bust-enlargement.

VARVARA SERGEEVNA. What?

NADEJDA PETROVNA. You, Nastia, always were a complete
  nincompoop, and now you've gone raving mad into the
  bargain. I'm trying to marry off my daughter, and all the
  time, under my very nose, you are abandoning yourself to
  lechery. Do I pay you wages for you to be enlarging your
  bust? Tell me?

VARVARA SERGEEVNA. Leave her alone, Mummy, please –
  it's quite interesting actually. Tell me, Nastia dear, can he
  really make them any bigger?

PAVEL SERGEEVICH. Varvara?

VARVARA SERGEEVNA. Well?

NASTIA. Yes. Loads.

PAVEL SERGEEVICH. Varvara?

VARVARA SERGEEVNA. How does he do it?

PAVEL SERGEEVICH. Varvara, don't be stupid!

NASTIA. I don't know how he does it exactly, but he's offered
  to do it for me personally. You know when I was living on
  Briussov, well just across the road there was a photo shop
  called 'Electric Chic'. So I got half-a-dozen photos done
  in this 'Electric Chic' – just for fun, you know. But, miss,
  those photos are so small and they're only your head and
  shoulders anyway. But then our Ivan Ivanovich is a

gentleman with an education in photography, so to say, he tells me yesterday: 'Anastasia Nikolaevna,' he says ' I will enlarge your bust for you.'

VARVARA SERGEEVNA. Damn, she got me all excited.

NADEJDA PETROVNA. What are you doing here anyway, you idiot? Get off back to the kitchen and be quiet.

NASTIA *exits.*

That brainless girl will be the death of me; my nerves are in shreds.

PAVEL SERGEEVICH. That is a minor problem, Mummy. More pressing is the question of proletarian relatives: I don't have any.

VARVARA SERGEEVNA. Oh, do stop going on: relatives, relatives . . .

PAVEL SERGEEVICH. Stop going on! What did you say – Oh, do stop going on? Why, say it again – OH, DO STOP GOING ON! Charming! – Oh, do stop going on! Just imagine, oh do stop going on, oh do stop going on, oh do stop going on: tell me again, what was that you just said?

VARVARA SERGEEVNA. Oh, do stop going on.

PAVEL SERGEEVICH. Oh, do stop going on?

VARVARA SERGEEVNA. Please.

PAVEL SERGEEVICH. These, Varvara, are my conditions. Number one. Find me at least one relative who is a fully paid-up member of the working classes, or reconcile yourself to a life of passionate chastity.

VARVARA SERGEEVNA. But where can I find them, Pavel?

PAVEL SERGEEVICH. Condition number one remains. Condition number two concerns the lodger, who goes around trying to enlarge the busts of other people's cooks – get rid of him. I refuse to live under the same roof.

VARVARA SERGEEVNA. But how can we possibly get rid of him, Pavel dear? It's against the law.

PAVEL SERGEEVICH. So you are saying you can't?

VARVARA SERGEEVNA. Exactly.

PAVEL SERGEEVICH. Then I'm saying – goodbye.

PAVEL *exits.*

NADEJDA PETROVNA. Please yourself, Varvara, but you're just going to have to find him some Communist relatives.

VARVARA SERGEEVNA. But even if I get him some proletarians, how are we going to get rid of Ivan Ivanovich?

NADEJDA PETROVNA. Noise, Varvara.

VARVARA SERGEEVNA. Noise?

NADEJDA PETROVNA. Ivan Ivanovich can't stand any unpleasant noise, Varvara. You could try singing, for example.

VARVARA SERGEEVNA. Tell me, Mummy, is he dark?

NADEJDA PETROVNA. Who? Ivan Ivanovich?

VARVARA SERGEEVNA. No. Smetanich's son.

NADEJDA PETROVNA. You're marrying a man, not a head of hair!

VARVARA SERGEEVNA. I don't even know his name.

NADEJDA PETROVNA. He is called Valerian.

VARVARA SERGEEVNA. Valerian Olympovich Smetanich. I'm satisfied.

NADEJDA PETROVNA. What do you mean – satisfied? Of course you're satisfied. Any sensible young lady would sink her teeth into a young man like Valerian Olympovich. What a soul he has, Varya! And what a body! And his father! Oh, his father! Just imagine, Varya, Olymp has been losing money ever since the revolution started, and somehow he never seems to get any poorer.

VARVARA SERGEEVNA. Mummy, do you think I ought to go to the hairdressers?

NADEJDA PETROVNA. Whatever for?

VARVARA SERGEEVNA. I always smell so nice after I've had my hair done.

NADEJDA PETROVNA. Go ahead, my little Varyushka!

VARVARA SERGEEVNA. Only please don't tell Valerian, Mummy, because I want him to think I smell that way all on my own.

VARVARA SERGEEVNA *exits.*

NADEJDA PETROVNA. Dear God above, what sort of a life is this we're living nowadays? Tell me, what sort of life is this? You nearly die of fright just trying to get your daughter married off. And you have to pay good money just for the privilege of living in your own house. What sort of life is this? People have changed so much. Not only are unmarried girls having babies, now they've even started smoking – in public! On the tram, men won't give their seats to a lady – not even to a priest. What sort of life is this we're leading now? Don't get me started. And look what they've done to the church, just look at what they've done to the church! In peacetime you could buy a candle for three kopecks and pray as long as you liked. And now they say they are going to make you pay a fine for each prayer. At that rate, an all-night service will bankrupt me. But I'm not so stupid. A true believer can always find a way to pray for free.

She puts a record on the gramophone; it plays an Orthodox chant. Enter TAMARA LEOPOLDOVNA, *followed by two* PORTERS *carrying a chest.*

Tamara Leopoldovna, is it you? Lord above, how lovely to see you! Good Heavens, Tamara Leopoldovna, are you moving in?

TAMARA LEOPOLDOVNA. Just don't ask, Nadejda Petrovna. (*To the* PORTERS.) Put it down there. Right.

NADEJDA PETROVNA. I don't quite understand, Tamara
Leopoldovna.

TAMARA LEOPOLDOVNA. It's all absolutely ghastly,
Nadejda Petrovna. (*To the* PORTERS.) That's all.

The PORTERS *exit.*

NADEJDA PETROVNA. You're frightening me, Tamara
Leopoldovna.

TAMARA LEOPOLDOVNA. Don't say that, Nadejda
Petrovna.

NADEJDA PETROVNA. Please sit down, Tamara Leopoldovna,
here in the armchair, here's a cushion. How is your health,
Tamara Leopoldovna, how is your health?

TAMARA LEOPOLDOVNA. Can't you see I'm white as a
sheet?

NADEJDA PETROVNA. Good Heavens, has something
untoward happened?

TAMARA LEOPOLDOVNA. It's too, too horrible! Just think
about it, Nadejda Petrovna, they're coming round to search
through the flat today. The barbarians! How can they treat a
lady like this, Nadejda Petrovna?

NADEJDA PETROVNA. Why are they going to search your
flat, the beasts?

TAMARA LEOPOLDOVNA. Dear Nadejda Petrovna, you are
so naive! What do you mean – why? Is there a reason for
anything these days?

NADEJDA PETROVNA. What times we are living in! What a
dreadful life we have now!

TAMARA LEOPOLDOVNA. Such a tremendous country –
then, quick as a flash, bang, revolution, and now look at us!
It's so shaming . . . and in front of foreigners, too. You
know, Nadejda Petrovna, my husband is always saying: 'If
they'd only postponed their revolution for another hundred
years, I could have accepted it.'

NADEJDA PETROVNA. So what are you going to do now, Tamara Leopoldovna?

TAMARA LEOPOLDOVNA. I have a favour to ask of you, Nadejda Petrovna, but I'm not quite sure you're up to it . . .

NADEJDA PETROVNA. For you, I'd do anything, Tamara Leopoldovna . . . you used to be our best client.

TAMARA LEOPOLDOVNA. Then would you look after this chest for me?

NADEJDA PETROVNA. Is that all?

TAMARA LEOPOLDOVNA. Well, you see, it's a rather dangerous chest.

NADEJDA PETROVNA. Dangerous?

TAMARA LEOPOLDOVNA. Just look inside. (*Opens it.*)

NADEJDA PETROVNA. Oh. It's only a dress. I thought it might be a bomb!

TAMARA LEOPOLDOVNA. Ah, Nadejda Petrovna, if only you knew whose dress it was.

NADEJDA PETROVNA. Isn't it yours, Tamara Leopoldovna?

TAMARA LEOPOLDOVNA. Don't ask, Nadejda Petrovna, I beg you, don't ask.

NADEJDA PETROVNA. But whose is it, Tamara Leopoldovna?

TAMARA LEOPOLDOVNA. Don't force me to tell you, Nadejda Petrovna.

NADEJDA PETROVNA. Please, Tamara Leopoldovna, tell me whose it is.

TAMARA LEOPOLDOVNA. Oh well, I suppose you'll have to know sooner or later, Nadejda Petrovna . . . This dress – the doors, Nadejda Petrovna – this dress belonged to . . . Alexandra Fedorovna!

NADEJDA PETROVNA. Oh, really? Which Alexandra
Fedorovna exactly? The midwife Alexandra Fedorovna, the
one who helped me with my dear Pavel?

TAMARA LEOPOLDOVNA. What midwife, Nadejda
Petrovna? – For goodness' sake – Alexandra Fedorovna, the
Empress!

NADEJDA PETROVNA. The Empress . . . oh, Tamara
Leopoldovna!

TAMARA LEOPOLDOVNA. Oh, Nadejda Petrovna! In a
word, if they find this dress at our place – we're done for!

A pause.

NADEJDA PETROVNA. This is absolutely appalling! You'd
better get rid of it – and a long way away, Tamara
Leopoldovna!

TAMARA LEOPOLDOVNA. Are you mad, Nadejda Petrovna?
Don't you realise, Nadejda Petrovna, that in this tiny chest
lies all that remains in Russia of Russia. And whoever's
going to save Russia these days, Nadejda Petrovna, if it isn't
you or me?

NADEJDA PETROVNA. How right you are, Tamara
Leopoldovna.

TAMARA LEOPOLDOVNA. In any case, Nadejda Petrovna,
sooner or later the French will send a new Tsar to Russia,
and then the dress might come in rather handy.

NADEJDA PETROVNA. Handy? How exactly?

TAMARA LEOPOLDOVNA. Well, I don't know exactly.
Maybe they'll give my husband a medal or a pension or
something.

NADEJDA PETROVNA. A pension? Do you think you could
put in a word for us, Tamara Leopoldovna?

TAMARA LEOPOLDOVNA. But of course, Nadejda
Petrovna, of course we will, for such heroics.

NADEJDA PETROVNA. I'll do my best for you, Tamara
Leopoldovna . . .

TAMARA LEOPOLDOVNA. Not for me, Nadejda Petrovna,
but for Russia.

A pause.

NADEJDA PETROVNA. Ah, Tamara Leopoldovna, will the
old days ever come back?

TAMARA LEOPOLDOVNA. My husband was saying to me
only this morning: 'Tamara, dear, have a look out of the
window, and tell me if those Soviets are still in power.'
I opened the curtains. 'I'm afraid they are my dear,' I had to
say, 'it seems they're still here.' 'Well, there's nothing more
to be done,' he says. 'Close the curtain, Tamara dear, and
we'll take another look tomorrow.'

NADEJDA PETROVNA. But when will this tomorrow come?

TAMARA LEOPOLDOVNA. Patience, Nadejda Petrovna,
patience. And in the meantime, hang on to this.

She takes out a gun.

NADEJDA PETROVNA. Good Heavens! A gun!

TAMARA LEOPOLDOVNA. Don't be afraid, Nadejda
Petrovna.

NADEJDA PETROVNA. But what if it goes off?

TAMARA LEOPOLDOVNA. If you don't touch it, Nadejda
Petrovna, it won't go off. But somehow it makes me feel
that the dress is safer. So look after it and trust in God.

NADEJDA PETROVNA. I certainly shall, Tamara
Leopoldovna. In fact, nowadays there's no one left in
Moscow that you can trust, apart from God, that is.

TAMARA LEOPOLDOVNA. Goodbye now, Nadejda
Petrovna, and just remember – not a word to anyone.

NADEJDA PETROVNA. I'll be as quiet as the grave, Tamara
Leopoldovna. God bless you!

TAMARA LEOPOLDOVNA *leaves.*

Dear God above, what sort of a life is this we're living nowadays? Tell me, what sort of life is this? I must pray.

She puts another record on the gramophone.

Lord, oh Lord, my Salvation and my Strength. Harken to my pitiful cries in this vale of tears.

The gramophone plays a noisy popular tune.

Heavens! Forgive me, Lord, it's the wrong record.

End of Act One.

ACT TWO

The GULIACHKINS' *flat.*

NASTIA *is reading a book.*

NASTIA (*reads*). ' "Baron," exclaimed the princess, "I did not say that I was in love with you. You forget yourself. Unhand me at once, sir!" "Princess," exclaimed the Baron, "take here my sword and run me through with it." ' Wow, this Baron's really desperate. ' "Unfortunate man," exclaimed the princess. "Do you really love me so much?" "Alas," exclaimed the Baron, "do I love you? Ask rather does a bird love its freedom!" ' Oh! How lovely! He's so passionate, this Baron! ' "Very well," exclaimed the Princess, "Here I cast off the sham veil of pretence!" And their lips met in exquisite ecstasy.'

God, what a life they had then! And to think it's all been . . . liquidated. I bet that if the government knew what the princessian way of life really was, they wouldn't have been so hasty.

She reads again.

'But love is just a mirage. Suddenly the bedroom door flew open and in stormed the Duke.' Oh dear, they're for it now. He's horrible, this Duke. He's so rude!

Enter IVAN IVANOVICH.

' "You varlet," exclaimed the Duke. "What are you doing in here?" '

IVAN IVANOVICH. Why shouldn't I come in, Anastasia Nikolaevna?

NASTIA. ' "Swine, does my honour count for nothing! Do you seek to ruin me?" '

IVAN IVANOVICH. Dear God, I wouldn't dream of such a thing, Anastasia Nikolaevna. Honestly, I wouldn't. My intentions were wholesome.

NASTIA. Oh, it's only you, Ivan Ivanovich!

IVAN IVANOVICH. Believe me, Anastasia Nikolaevna, to me a lady's honour is a thing of mystery and delight. A priceless ruby I would defend with my life. However, Anastasia Nikolaevna, I do feel a modern need to lean upon a female soul.

NASTIA. Whatever are you saying, Ivan Ivanovich?

IVAN IVANOVICH. Please try to understand me. Anastasia Nikolaevna, I'm a single man. No one darns *my* underwear. Besides, a fine girl like you could drive any chap to distraction.

NASTIA. Ivan Ivanovich, may I remind you that I am a nice girl, and consequently do not know what you are driving at.

IVAN IVANOVICH. Please, don't be put off by my moustache, Anastasia Nikolaevna. Deep down I'm just a big baby.

NASTIA. Why, Ivan Ivanovich, a large moustache is a gift from Heaven. Only you shouldn't wear it upside down, Ivan Ivanovich.

IVAN IVANOVICH. What do you mean, upside down?

NASTIA. Well, Ivan Ivanovich, yours is all bent down, see, but it would look ever so much nicer if it stuck up, Ivan Ivanovich – altogether more pleasing to the eye.

IVAN IVANOVICH. A man's moustache, Anastasia Nikolaevna, needs the female touch. All neglected it will sink and droop, but a woman's fingers can tempt it upwards to an idyll of eternal bliss.

NASTIA. Oh, Ivan Ivanovich, I wouldn't know how.

IVAN IVANOVICH. You'll get the hang of it, Anastasia Nikolaevna, I'm sure you will.

NASTIA. No, really. I couldn't.

IVAN IVANOVICH. Just give it a go.

NASTIA. I'd feel all peculiar redirecting a strange man's moustache.

IVAN IVANOVICH. Well then, perhaps you could do it just out of curiosity, Anastasia Nikolaevna.

NASTIA. Oh well. Okey-dokey, but just out of curiosity, mind, Ivan Ivanovich. And don't you go getting any ideas now.

IVAN IVANOVICH. Dear Anastasia Nikolaevna, I never have ideas.

NASTIA. All righty, here we go. Oh. (*Pause.*) I don't seem to be able to get it up at all.

IVAN IVANOVICH. Not even a bit?

NASTIA. You must have been born like that.

IVAN IVANOVICH. Try licking your fingers, Anastasia Nikolaevna.

NASTIA. Okey-dokey.

IVAN IVANOVICH. Believe me, Anastasia Nikolaevna, your touch sears right through my follicles down to the embers of my very heart. (*Tries to embrace her.*)

NASTIA. Baron, you forget yourself.

IVAN IVANOVICH. Forgive me, Anastasia Nikolaevna, that was a rush of passion I just had. But never forget, with your love I would fear nothing. Say you'll share your fate with mine, and let's shake hands on it.

NASTIA. But I don't know anything about you. You could be anybody – maybe you've even got kiddies somewhere.

IVAN IVANOVICH. Children are not a disgrace, Anastasia Nikolaevna, just bad luck. However, if you have anything against my outer appearance . . .

NASTIA. Oh no, I've seen a lot worse.

IVAN IVANOVICH. Maybe the way I dress leaves something to be desired . . .

NASTIA. Oh no!

IVAN IVANOVICH. If you'd care to examine my tie, Anastasia Nikolaevna, you will find I am no stranger to style.

NASTIA. Your tie is very beautiful but why have you stuck noodles on it?

IVAN IVANOVICH. What do you mean – noodles?

NASTIA. Here, Ivan Ivanovich, noodles.

IVAN IVANOVICH. The swine!

NASTIA. 'Exclaimed the Duke.'

IVAN IVANOVICH. What?

NASTIA. Sorry, it was automatic. But, pardon me, to whom did you so refer?

IVAN IVANOVICH. What do you mean, to whom? To Pavel Sergeevich, of course.

NASTIA. Pavel Sergeevich!

IVAN IVANOVICH. By the way, could you tell me exactly when it was that Pavel Sergeevich managed to join the Party?

NASTIA. He never joined the Party.

IVAN IVANOVICH. What do you mean, never joined?

NASTIA. Just that.

IVAN IVANOVICH. Very interesting. Tell me, quickly, where did you put the noodles from my tie?

NASTIA. On the floor, Ivan Ivanovich.

IVAN IVANOVICH. On the floor? Where exactly?

NASTIA. I don't think that's a very good idea, Ivan Ivanovich
– eating noodles from under your shoe is ever so bad for
your hygiene.

IVAN IVANOVICH. Please find the noodles and return them
to me as soon as possible! I'll be right back.

IVAN IVANOVICH *exits.*

NASTIA. He was expressing his feelings so delicately, and
suddenly, there you go – noodles. Here's some. Funny, isn't
it? That such a tiny piece of noodle could shatter all your
dreams?

Re-enter IVAN IVANOVICH *with the pot on his head.*

IVAN IVANOVICH. Well, have you found the noodles?

NASTIA. Heavens above, Ivan Ivanovich, why have you got
that pot on your head?

IVAN IVANOVICH. Sh! Sh! For goodness' sake, don't tell
anyone I ever took it *off.* Everyone's got to think that it's
always been on my head.

NASTIA. What do you mean, always on your head? Tell me,
Ivan Ivanovich, do you normally live in a pot?

IVAN IVANOVICH. I'm forced to – for the time being. But
where are the noodles, Anastasia Nikolaevna?

NASTIA. Honestly, Ivan Ivanovich, you ought wipe the dirt off
first.

IVAN IVANOVICH. On the contrary, Anastasia Nikolaevna,
the filthier the better. This is evidence. Let impartial justice
see how former property-owners still grind the proletarian
face in the dirt – or at least in noodles.

NASTIA. Where are you going looking like that, Ivan
Ivanovich?

IVAN IVANOVICH. To the Militia, Anastasia Nikolaevna, to
the Militia!

IVAN IVANOVICH *runs out.*

NASTIA. To the Militia? Ivan Ivanovich! Ivan Ivanovich! If the Militia catch him in a hat like that, they won't let him go in a hurry.

Enter VARVARA SERGEEVNA *and the* ORGAN-GRINDER.

VARVARA SERGEEVNA. Come in. Come in! Just stand over there, please, and play at that wall. Off you go! Why don't you play?

ORGAN-GRINDER. Of course, it's all the same to me, but wouldn't you rather I went out in the yard, and then you could listen to me through the window?

VARVARA SERGEEVNA. What?

ORGAN-GRINDER. Well, I'm not big on conversation, and I'm orchestrated for the outdoors.

VARVARA SERGEEVNA. So why did you agree to come with me?

ORGAN-GRINDER. Well, I thought it was for a big birthday do or maybe just some everyday drunken revelry. But it's a bit peculiar, just the two of us like this, one on one, I can't play like this.

VARVARA SERGEEVNA. Please understand that I am trying to get rid of someone.

ORGAN-GRINDER. I can see that you are not altogether stable, miss. Never mind, nowadays lots of people are a sandwich short of a picnic on account of the new regime.

VARVARA SERGEEVNA. My dear man, I am perfectly sane. I merely wish to drive out a lodger.

ORGAN-GRINDER. Oh, a lodger, is it? Well then, that's a different kettle of fish. Why exactly do you want to drive him out, miss?

VARVARA SERGEEVNA. He's nothing but a lout. Can you believe that all because of him I shall die a virgin?

ORGAN-GRINDER. Really? How's that then, that he's making you into a virgin, miss?

VARVARA SERGEEVNA. Presumably you are unaware that I am engaged to be married. But my brother, Pavel Sergeevich, issued me with an ultimatum this very morning. 'If you don't get rid of the lodger,' he declared, 'I'll make sure you never get married!'

ORGAN-GRINDER. Well, that would be a pity, miss, since the state of chastity is like having a dog in a mangle: no one gets much fun out of it.

VARVARA SERGEEVNA. Indeed. So we, me and Mummy that is, have decided to drive out the lodger by playing loud music.

ORGAN-GRINDER. Right. What sort of music did you have in mind then, miss?

VARVARA SERGEEVNA. Church music.

ORGAN-GRINDER. Beg pardon, miss, but I don't play church music. My instrument is strictly Soviet.

VARVARA SERGEEVNA. Very well, play whatever you can, but make it as loud as possible.

The ORGAN-GRINDER *plays,* VARVARA SERGEEVNA *sings.* NASTIA*'s voice is heard:*

NASTIA (*off*). Stop, stop, I'm coming.

In rushes NASTIA.

Thank Heavens, she's alive, look, she's alive! Mary, Mother of God, she's really alive.

VARVARA SERGEEVNA. Who? Who? Who is alive? Who is alive?

NASTIA. You, Varvara Sergeevna, you're alive, really alive.

VARVARA SERGEEVNA. Have you gone mad?

NASTIA. But how is it possible, Varvara Sergeevna? I was in the kitchen and the downstairs cook says to me: 'Your

Varvara Sergeevna's making such a racket, I reckon someone must be murdering her.'

VARVARA SERGEEVNA. What do you mean – racket? I was singing. You are a complete idiot. Well, that's enough talking, now let's dance.

NASTIA. What? What's this?

VARVARA SERGEEVNA. Dance, I say.

NASTIA. I don't do dancing, miss.

VARVARA SERGEEVNA. What do you mean, you don't do dancing? We pay you to scrub the floors, you hardly have the right to refuse something artistic. If you are told to 'dance' it means 'dance'. Do play, play, sir, please. Sing, sing louder.

They sing and dance.

Stop, stop, quickly. Nastia, come over here. Smell me, here. Tell me, have I evaporated? Well! What? How is it? Do I still have an aroma?

NASTIA. You do smell a bit, miss.

VARVARA SERGEEVNA. Thank God. After all this dancing, the scent from the hairdresser's might have worn off. And I'm saving it for Valerian Olympich.

ORGAN-GRINDER. I think that's him packing his bags already, miss, and I shouldn't wonder – I'm all covered in sweat.

NASTIA. Who is packing?

VARVARA SERGEEVNA. Ivan Ivanovich.

NASTIA. Ivan Ivanovich? He's not here.

VARVARA SERGEEVNA. Where is he?

NASTIA. He's . . .

VARVARA SERGEEVNA. Yes.

NASTIA. Ivan Ivanovich . . .

VARVARA SERGEEVNA. Yes, yes, him! Where is he?

NASTIA. He's in a pot.

VARVARA SERGEEVNA. Where?

NASTIA. I mean . . . I wanted to say he must be out . . .

VARVARA SERGEEVNA. We've wasted all our energy.

ORGAN-GRINDER. No, we haven't!

VARVARA SERGEEVNA. How do you mean, 'No, we
haven't'?

ORGAN-GRINDER. Maybe you've been singing away for
nothing, miss, but you're contractually obliged to pay me
anyway.

VARVARA SERGEEVNA. Wait, who are you?

ORGAN-GRINDER. What do you mean, who am I?

VARVARA SERGEEVNA. Just, who are you?

ORGAN-GRINDER. I'm . . . a People's Artist.

VARVARA SERGEEVNA. I didn't mean that! Tell me, are
you a member of the working classes?

ORGAN-GRINDER. No, I'm artistic – I taught myself to play.

VARVARA SERGEEVNA. Oh, what a shame.

ORGAN-GRINDER. What do you need to know for?

VARVARA SERGEEVNA. Oh, it's not for me, it's for my
brother. I promised him I'd find him some relatives from the
working class.

ORGAN-GRINDER. Relatives?

VARVARA SERGEEVNA. Precisely. You see, they're going
to visit him from the Party today, and he's not got a single
working-class relative.

ORGAN-GRINDER. Why didn't you get him some earlier, miss?

VARVARA SERGEEVNA. Because he didn't need any till now.

ORGAN-GRINDER. So what are you going to do about it, miss?

VARVARA SERGEEVNA. I shall just have to go and rent some proletarians. But where can one find them?

ORGAN-GRINDER. Oh, that's easy enough.

VARVARA SERGEEVNA. Could you find me some?

ORGAN-GRINDER. Why, yes, I suppose so.

VARVARA SERGEEVNA. You know, we've made them some vol-au-vents and there's a selection of different bonbons. The working classes would be most welcome.

ORGAN-GRINDER. That's okay for the body, but what have you got for the soul?

VARVARA SERGEEVNA. What do you mean, for the soul?

ORGAN-GRINDER. Well, like for example, will there be any, for example, booze?

VARVARA SERGEEVNA. Of course there will.

ORGAN-GRINDER. There will?

VARVARA SERGEEVNA. Of course.

ORGAN-GRINDER. You know, miss, my memory's got something shocking.

VARVARA SERGEEVNA. Why?

ORGAN-GRINDER. Just imagine, I clean forgot I happen to come from the working class myself.

VARVARA SERGEEVNA. Oh, really!

ORGAN-GRINDER. Miss, in what kind of quantity would you be requiring these relatives?

VARVARA SERGEEVNA. I think three should do it, one relative per Communist guest.

ORGAN-GRINDER. I reckon that'd set you back a bottle per each relative.

VARVARA SERGEEVNA. Done. Then I'll be expecting you all five-ish.

ORGAN-GRINDER. We'll be there and don't you worry, miss.

NASTIA *and the* ORGAN-GRINDER *exit.*

VARVARA SERGEEVNA. What a life! Worry, worry, worry and no fun. Once a month you bargain your way into the hairdresser's, that's the closest to glamour you get. Mummy won't even let me go to church, she says you can get murdered there. All the baths are full of riff-raff now, so it's not interesting to have a wash any more. Where's a nice girl from the intelligentsia supposed to go these days? I wonder if Valerian Olympovich will go for me or not? I think he will. My soul is beautiful, they say, and my eyelashes, too, apparently. Also, I have a smile to die for, but I don't seem to be able to fit it all into this tiny mirror.

Enter PAVEL SERGEEVICH.

PAVEL SERGEEVICH. Why are you pulling that silly face, Varvara?

VARVARA SERGEEVNA. Why, doesn't it suit me?

PAVEL SERGEEVICH. I suppose it doesn't really matter with a face like yours. But perhaps it's about time you started thinking about your brother – does your face suit him?

VARVARA SERGEEVNA. It's not a 'face', Pavel dear, it's a smile.

PAVEL SERGEEVICH. A smile! Listen to me, Varvara, if you dare to smile like that at any of my guests, I shall . . . denounce you!

VARVARA SERGEEVNA. You can't denounce me.

PAVEL SERGEEVICH. Oh yes I can, and not only that but I'll also dishonour you for the rest of your life.

VARVARA SERGEEVNA. How can you dishonour me?

PAVEL SERGEEVICH. Very easily: I'll tell them you are not my sister but my aunt.

VARVARA SERGEEVNA. Pavel, I've managed to find you a relative, and you go on being horrid. You're so ungrateful!

PAVEL SERGEEVICH. You've found someone? Is he a worker?

VARVARA SERGEEVNA. He is exquisitely proletarian.

PAVEL SERGEEVICH. What sort of work does he actually do?

VARVARA SERGEEVNA. The manual variety. (*Cheerfully.*) So are the Communists actually coming round, then?

PAVEL SERGEEVICH. Yes, they most certainly are. Comrade Utkin said he'd bring them over himself.

VARVARA SERGEEVNA. So you're a proper Party man now?

PAVEL SERGEEVICH. To the tips of my fingers. I've even got a briefcase, look, but I haven't got the membership card yet.

VARVARA SERGEEVNA. Oh, I shouldn't worry, Pavel, with a briefcase like that they'd let you in anywhere.

PAVEL SERGEEVICH. So a new life is dawning.

VARVARA SERGEEVNA. Look, Pavel – a chest.

PAVEL SERGEEVICH. Where is there a chest?

VARVARA SERGEEVNA. Here, this chest.

PAVEL SERGEEVICH. Yes, that's a chest all right.

VARVARA SERGEEVNA. How peculiar.

PAVEL SERGEEVICH. It is quite peculiar.

VARVARA SERGEEVNA. What do you think's inside?

PAVEL SERGEEVICH. Let's take a look.

VARVARA SERGEEVNA. It's locked, Pavel.

PAVEL SERGEEVICH. Yes, it's locked.

VARVARA SERGEEVNA. How peculiar.

PAVEL SERGEEVICH. Yes, that is very peculiar. Particularly because Mummy spends all her time whining that she's got nothing left. Just ask her: 'Where are Daddy's trousers?' 'We ate them, Pavel dear,' she says. 'We ate them. In 1918 we traded everything we had for flour and ate it.' Or just try asking her for money. 'What money could we possibly have?' she says. 'In 1918 they took everything.' 'So how are we managing to live, Mummy?' 'We manage to live, Pavel dear,' she says, 'by eating through Daddy's trousers.' What kind of trousers did Daddy wear, I ask you, that an entire family could survive by eating them?

VARVARA SERGEEVNA. Presumably Mummy's got something else hidden, besides Daddy's trousers.

PAVEL SERGEEVICH. Well, there must be something in there, Varvara dear, otherwise why would she keep it locked?

VARVARA SERGEEVNA. Pavel, the lock isn't very strong.

PAVEL SERGEEVICH. No, and it's quite loose, too.

VARVARA SERGEEVNA. I expect you could open a lock like that with a fork.

PAVEL SERGEEVICH. Oh no, Varvara. How could you? A fork? Definitely not. But with a nail, now . . . What happens if we're caught?

VARVARA SERGEEVNA. Who could suspect us, Pavel? We look so respectable. No one would ever dream it could be us.

PAVEL SERGEEVICH. But what if Mummy finds out?

VARVARA SERGEEVNA. Mummy will only think it's that idiot Nastia, on the well-known principle that all cooks are thieves.

PAVEL SERGEEVICH. You know, I never thought it before, but that Nastia's got such a strange glint in her eyes, she might actually *be* a thief – well, all things considered . . . she probably is . . .

VARVARA SERGEEVNA. Let's face it, Pavel, she definitely is a thief.

PAVEL SERGEEVICH. There are so many dishonest people around these days, you lose count. (*Puts a nail into the lock, tries to open it.*)

Enter NADEJDA PETROVNA. PAVEL *and* VARVARA *hide behind the chest.*

NADEJDA PETROVNA. Dear Mother of God, someone is at the Empress's dress. Burglars! Thieves. Help! Help! I'll shoot!

NADEJDA *aims the gun.*

VARVARA SERGEEVNA. Help . . . Thieves . . .

PAVEL SERGEEVICH. Get down!

NADEJDA PETROVNA. It's either burglars or Bolsheviks.

PAVEL SERGEEVICH (*from behind the chest*). Comrade!

NADEJDA PETROVNA. Oh my God! They *are* Bolsheviks. (*To the gun.*) Please don't go off, please don't go off!

The gun goes off.

PAVEL SERGEEVICH. Varvara, pinch me, am I still alive?

VARVARA SERGEEVNA. I think so.

NADEJDA PETROVNA. We're finished. That's absolutely it.

PAVEL SERGEEVICH. Are you all right?

VARVARA SERGEEVNA. I think most of me is still alive.

NADEJDA PETROVNA. They'll arrest me, the swine, they will.

PAVEL SERGEEVICH. Comrade, please understand that we are mere children – the Tender Seedlings of Socialism.

NADEJDA PETROVNA. Tamara Leopoldovna forced me to hide the dress, honestly – it was all Tamara Leopoldovna's fault.

PAVEL SERGEEVICH. Ask yourself, comrade, how will shooting us help build Socialism? Mummy will be home in a minute, and you can talk to her.

NADEJDA PETROVNA. Hang on: are you Bolsheviks or are you burglars?

PAVEL SERGEEVICH. Well, we're not exactly Bolsheviks.

NADEJDA PETROVNA. Thank God, they're only burglars! Help! Thieves!

PAVEL SERGEEVICH. Mummy!

NADEJDA PETROVNA. Help me! Careful or I'll shoot!

PAVEL SERGEEVICH. Calm down, Mummy, it's me, Pavel.

NADEJDA PETROVNA. Is it really you?

PAVEL SERGEEVICH. Me, Mummy.

VARVARA SERGEEVNA. It's him, Mummy, it's Pavel.

PAVEL SERGEEVICH. Can't you see for yourself, Mummy?

NADEJDA PETROVNA. How can I possibly see, Pavel, when I've got both my eyes shut.

PAVEL SERGEEVICH. Open your eyes immediately, Mummy, or there'll be a catastrophe.

NADEJDA PETROVNA. How can I open my eyes, Pavel dear? It's about to go off again.

PAVEL SERGEEVICH. Mummy, you're aiming at me again. Turn it towards yourself, the hole, Mummy, it's got a hole, turn the hole towards yourself, Mummy, aim at yourself, aim at yourself, I'm telling you, otherwise you'll shoot your own children, God Almighty save us!

NADEJDA PETROVNA. It's going to explode in my hands, Pavel dear, I swear to you, it's going to explode.

VARVARA SERGEEVNA. Mummy, put it down somewhere, slowly and calmly.

NADEJDA PETROVNA. I can feel it, Pavel dear, it's going to go off. (*She drops the gun.*)

PAVEL SERGEEVICH. You're turning the flat into a battlefield. Now kindly explain to me, Mummy: where did you get the gun?

NADEJDA PETROVNA. Tamara Leopoldovna gave it to me, Pavel dear.

PAVEL SERGEEVICH. And why, pray, did Tamara Leopoldovna give you a gun?

NADEJDA PETROVNA. For the self-defence of the dress, Pavel dear.

VARVARA SERGEEVNA. The dress?

PAVEL SERGEEVICH. What dress?

NADEJDA PETROVNA. The dress, Pavel dear, which once upon a time contained the entire country.

PAVEL SERGEEVICH. Where is it now, Mummy?

NADEJDA PETROVNA. In the chest, Pavel dear.

PAVEL SERGEEVICH. How does it all fit in?

NADEJDA PETROVNA. Well, they took the country out first.

PAVEL SERGEEVICH. Whose dress is it, Mummy?

Pause.

NADEJDA PETROVNA. First, swear to Almighty God that you won't tell a soul, because I myself have sworn to Almighty God that I won't tell a soul.

VARVARA SERGEEVNA. I swear to Almighty God, Mummy, I'll tell no one.

NADEJDA PETROVNA. And you, Pavel dear?

PAVEL SERGEEVICH. I'm a Communist. I can't possibly swear to God.

VARVARA SERGEEVNA. Whisper, Pavel, the Communists won't hear.

PAVEL SERGEEVICH (*whispers*). I swear to Almighty God I won't tell a soul.

NADEJDA PETROVNA. This dress, my children – (*Crosses herself.*) – belonged to Her Imperial Majesty, the Empress Alexandra Fedorovna.

Pause.

PAVEL SERGEEVICH. Forgive me for being blunt, Mummy, but that is a complete lie.

NADEJDA PETROVNA. Pavel dear, I'm not lying any more than I do at confession! Look for yourself. (*Unlocks the chest.*)

PAVEL SERGEEVICH. But, Mummy, it's absolutely magnificent.

VARVARA SERGEEVNA. Gosh! The dressmaker was really brave to run up a frock for the Empress.

PAVEL SERGEEVICH. You are a fool, Varvara. An Empress's gown isn't run up by some little dressmaker.

VARVARA SERGEEVNA. Then who makes them?

PAVEL SERGEEVICH. A general's wife, maybe, or some Grand Duchess or other.

VARVARA SERGEEVNA. I'd love to see, Mummy, how it looks on someone.

PAVEL SERGEEVICH. There are no more women like that left in Russia.

VARVARA SERGEEVNA. What about me?

PAVEL SERGEEVICH. You haven't quite got the figure for it. But what about Nastia! Look, Mummy, it'll fit Nastia perfectly.

NADEJDA PETROVNA. Don't be ridiculous, she's just a cook!

PAVEL SERGEEVICH. Yes, it will fit! Yes! Nastia! Nastia! Nastia!

EVERYONE. Nastia!

Enter NASTIA.

NASTIA. Here I am!

VARVARA SERGEEVNA. Quick, put this dress on!

NASTIA *and* VARVARA SERGEEVNA *run off with the dress.*

NADEJDA PETROVNA. You know, Pavel dear, Tamara Leopoldovna promised to get me a pension.

PAVEL SERGEEVICH. A pension for what?

NADEJDA PETROVNA. For saving Russia.

PAVEL SERGEEVICH. What do you mean, for saving Russia? To begin with, the Communists wouldn't dream of letting anyone save Russia.

NADEJDA PETROVNA. Who's asking them, Pavel dear? Anyway, the French are about to send us a new Tsar.

PAVEL SERGEEVICH. What do you mean, a new Tsar? Do you know what you are saying, Mummy? If Russia goes Tsarist again, I'll be hanged along with all the other Communists and it won't be so easy convincing them I only did it to stop my sister dying a virgin.

NADEJDA PETROVNA. But Pavel, just think about it – a pension!

PAVEL SERGEEVICH. What good will your pension do me if I'm dead, Mummy?

NADEJDA PETROVNA. What if they make a statue of you?

PAVEL SERGEEVICH. A statue?

NADEJDA PETROVNA. That's what they do for heroes. For the Edification of Posterity.

PAVEL SERGEEVICH. This dress just means I can't join the Party, that's all, Mummy.

NADEJDA PETROVNA. Of course you can join the Party. How else are we going to get our dear Varvara married off?

PAVEL SERGEEVICH. You seem to forget, Mummy, that the Tsarists will torture me to death for being a Bolshevik.

NADEJDA PETROVNA. How could they if you have the dress?

PAVEL SERGEEVICH. And the Bolsheviks will torture me to death for having the dress.

NADEJDA PETROVNA. But how can they if you join the Party?

PAVEL SERGEEVICH. It appears, Mummy, that under either regime I'm immortal. Just think about that statue! Tourists will come to Red Square. 'Whose is that statue?' they'll ask eagerly. 'Could it be Peter the Great or some athlete perhaps?' 'Think bigger, comrades,' the guide will smile. 'That is the monument to Pavel Sergeevich Guliachkin.'

Enter VARVARA SERGEEVNA.

VARVARA SERGEEVNA. Mummy! It's a perfect fit!

NADEJDA PETROVNA. What! Where is she?

VARVARA SERGEEVNA. She's coming.

PAVEL SERGEEVICH. If the real Empress came in now, what should one say? – 'Good afternoon' or 'Honoured to see you'?

NADEJDA PETROVNA. You don't say 'Good afternoon' to an Empress. You shout 'Hurrah'.

VARVARA SERGEEVNA. Will you hurry up?

NASTIA (*off*). I'm coming!

PAVEL SERGEEVICH. God, it's only the cook, but I'm still nervous.

Enter NASTIA *in the Empress's dress.*

EVERYONE. Hurrah, Your Majesty!

NADEJDA PETROVNA. Just like the real one, just like the real one! Hurrah, Your Majesty!

VARVARA SERGEEVNA. It's magnificent, I've got goose-pimples, Mummy.

NADEJDA PETROVNA. The train, the train is dragging up all the dust behind her.

PAVEL SERGEEVICH. Mummy, allow me. (PAVEL *carries the train.*)

NADEJDA PETROVNA. Just like the real one, just like the real one!

VARVARA SERGEEVNA. Now Pavel, let's sit her down on the throne.

PAVEL SERGEEVICH. Please be seated, Your Majesty.

They sit NASTIA *on the chair.*

NADEJDA PETROVNA. Just like the real one, just like the real one!

NASTIA. Here, what's this funny lump I'm sitting on?

NADEJDA PETROVNA. Just like the real one! Just like the . . . Run for your lives!

VARVARA SERGEEVNA. What?

NASTIA. What's the matter?

NADEJDA PETROVNA. Nastia, don't move an inch! I beg you, in the name of dear God in Heaven, don't move a muscle . . . you are sitting on a loaded gun.

NASTIA. A gun?! Help! Murder!

NADEJDA PETROVNA. Nastia, keep still!

PAVEL SERGEEVICH. Pretend you're a statue, Nastia, or we'll all die horribly!

VARVARA SERGEEVNA. If you so much as breathe, Nastia dear, it'll go off.

NASTIA. Oh no, I'm coming over all peculiar!

NADEJDA PETROVNA. Don't move, I'm warning you!

PAVEL SERGEEVICH. Nastia, can you possibly feel around a bit with . . . *that* part of your body . . . and tell which direction the gun is pointing in?

NASTIA. I'm ever so sorry, Pavel Sergeevich, but that part of my body has gone somewhat numb.

PAVEL SERGEEVICH. Mummy, I can't live under artillery fire, we'll have to move out immediately.

NASTIA. Pavel Sergeevich, you're not going to leave me here all alone, sitting on a loaded gun?

NADEJDA PETROVNA. Do try not to shake, Nastia dear, it's got seven bullets left.

NASTIA. Oh no! I just felt the trigger with something!

PAVEL SERGEEVICH. Dive under the table! Get down! It'll shoot out horizontally! This is all your fault, Mummy.

NADEJDA PETROVNA. No, it's all stupid Varvara's fault, Pavel dear. She told us to sit her on the throne, so we did.

The doorbell rings.

Good Heavens, there's someone at the door.

VARVARA SERGEEVNA. It must be Olymp Valerianovich.

NADEJDA PETROVNA. Cover her with something quickly. Cover her up quickly, and I'll see who it is.

NADEJDA PETROVNA *exits.*

PAVEL SERGEEVICH. Varvara, get some old curtains or a bit of carpet. Cover her over, more, more, I'm telling you, cover her completely . . .

He throws the carpet over NASTIA. *Re-enter* NADEJDA PETROVNA, *with* OLYMP VALERIANOVICH SMETANICH *and* VALERIAN OLYMPOVICH, *his son.*

NADEJDA PETROVNA. Please come in, Olymp Valerianovich, please come through here.

OLYMP VALERIANOVICH. So this is it, is it?

NADEJDA PETROVNA. Yes, this is it, Olymp Valerianovich, and this is my dear daughter, Varvara.

OLYMP VALERIANOVICH. Enchanted to meet you, mademoiselle.

VARVARA SERGEEVNA. Oh, it's nothing really!

OLYMP VALERIANOVICH. Valerian!

VALERIAN OLYMPOVICH. Yes, Papa?

OLYMP VALERIANOVICH. Say hello to Varvara Sergeevna!

VALERIAN OLYMPOVICH. I'm charmed.

VARVARA SERGEEVNA. I don't mind if I do!

NADEJDA PETROVNA. And this is my dear Party member son, Pavel.

OLYMP VALERIANOVICH. Oh, so you've already joined the Party, young man? And when exactly did you join?

PAVEL SERGEEVICH. You know, I had the intention . . . had the first inklings, so to say, all the way back in 1905 . . . because, as our beloved teacher Engels used to say . . .

VALERIAN OLYMPOVICH. Oh, what did he say?

PAVEL SERGEEVICH. That . . . well . . . he said lots of things, so it's rather hard to remember them all.

OLYMP VALERIANOVICH. Tell me, young man, how did you happen to join the Party? What were your reasons? Was it your political convictions or because . . . ?

NADEJDA PETROVNA. Whatever reasons you prefer, Olymp Valerianovich.

OLYMP VALERIANOVICH. Well, let's put it another way, do you 'look after' anyone, young man?

PAVEL SERGEEVICH. What do you mean, exactly, please, by 'look after'?

OLYMP VALERIANOVICH. 'Look after' . . . how can I explain it to . . . this is . . .

NADEJDA PETROVNA. Please come through to the other room, Olymp Valerianovich.

OLYMP VALERIANOVICH. Well, you know, businesses sometimes need 'protecting', from riff-raff.

PAVEL SERGEEVICH. Protecting businesses?

OLYMP VALERIANOVICH. Well, yes. You know. You scratch their back, and they scratch yours. Know what I mean?

NADEJDA PETROVNA. He's a personal friend of Comrade Utkin, Olymp Valerianovich.

OLYMP VALERIANOVICH. Who's Comrade Utkin?

NADEJDA PETROVNA. 'Who's Comrade Utkin?' But he's famous. Can you imagine, three of his relatives are Communists?

PAVEL SERGEEVICH. And they're all dropping round today, Olymp Valerianovich.

OLYMP VALERIANOVICH. Here? Now? Three Communists? Valerian!

VALERIAN OLYMPOVICH. Yes, Papa?

OLYMP VALERIANOVICH. Quick, put on your 'Friends of the Air Forces Society' medal, and remember to keep your opinions to yourself.

VALERIAN OLYMPOVICH. I'll put the medal on, Papa, but I don't have any opinions: I'm an anarchist.

OLYMP VALERIANOVICH. Kids like ours, Nadejda Petrovna, always have too much to say – they're always repeating what they hear at home. But tell me, Nadejda Petrovna, why do you keep your carpet on the armchair?

NADEJDA PETROVNA. It's . . . it's to . . . please come through to the other room and let's leave the young people together.

PAVEL SERGEEVICH, NADEJDA PETROVNA *and* OLYMP VALERIANOVICH *exit.*

VALERIAN OLYMPOVICH. Tell me, mademoiselle, do you play the piano?

VARVARA SERGEEVNA. I don't know, I never had the chance to try.

VALERIAN OLYMPOVICH. Have you noticed, mademoiselle, what the Soviet regime has done to art?

VARVARA SERGEEVNA. Oh no, I'm so sorry, I wasn't paying attention.

VALERIAN OLYMPOVICH. Just imagine, nowadays they treat artists like taxi-drivers.

VARVARA SERGEEVNA. What a shame!

NASTIA. It's going to go off!

VALERIAN OLYMPOVICH. What's that? Who said 'It's going to go off'?

VARVARA SERGEEVNA. Um, it was me.

VALERIAN OLYMPOVICH. You! . . . What's going to go off, exactly?

VARVARA SERGEEVNA. Um . . . artists, they're going to go off, if they carry on like that.

VALERIAN OLYMPOVICH. Really! And tell me, mademoiselle, what do you think about Einstein's Theory of Relativity?

VARVARA SERGEEVNA. It was on in the local cinema, but Pavel said that it's not really drama, just empty spectacle.

VALERIAN OLYMPOVICH. Do you often go to the cinema?

VARVARA SERGEEVNA. Certainly not, that would be rather improper.

VALERIAN OLYMPOVICH. Why would it be improper?

VARVARA SERGEEVNA. What, with all those strange men in the dark?

NASTIA *sneezes from underneath the carpet.*

VALERIAN OLYMPOVICH. Who's that sneezing?

VARVARA SERGEEVNA. Valerian Olympovich!

VALERIAN OLYMPOVICH. I asked who was that sneezing?

VARVARA SERGEEVNA. I . . . I was going to say . . .

VALERIAN OLYMPOVICH. Who's that sneezing?

VARVARA SERGEEVNA. I mean I . . . I . . . wanted to ask you . . .

VALERIAN OLYMPOVICH. Ask me what? There *is* someone sneezing!

VARVARA SERGEEVNA. Dear God above, what was I going to ask? Oh yes, you . . . you don't seem to be wearing any pince-nez?

VALERIAN OLYMPOVICH. No. My eyesight is perfect.

VARVARA SERGEEVNA. Oh, what a pity, it really suits a man to wear pince-nez.

NASTIA *sneezes loudly.*

VALERIAN OLYMPOVICH. Somebody is sneezing again.

VARVARA SERGEEVNA. It's . . . it's me.

VALERIAN OLYMPOVICH. You?

VARVARA SERGEEVNA. Let's go into the other room, Valerian Olympovich.

VALERIAN OLYMPOVICH. Wouldn't it be better to stay here for a bit, Varvara Sergeevna?

VARVARA SERGEEVNA. For the love of God, let's go to the other room, Valerian Olympovich!

VALERIAN OLYMPOVICH. Then allow me to offer you my hand, mademoiselle.

VARVARA SERGEEVNA. Oh, but this is so dreadfully sudden, Valerian Olympovich! It's so, so embarrassing, but, oh, all right, I accept.

VALERIAN OLYMPOVICH. But, Varvara Sergeevna, I didn't mean . . .

VARVARA SERGEEVNA. Shush shush shush, Valerian Olympovich, I know perfectly well what you meant, you naughty boy, but you'd better speak to Mummy about this first. Mummy!

VALERIAN OLYMPOVICH. Now I understand what they mean by 'hooked'.

VARVARA SERGEEVNA. Oh, he's so impulsive!

Re-enter NADEJDA PETROVNA*,* OLYMP VALERIANOVICH *and* PAVEL SERGEEVICH.

NADEJDA PETROVNA. Please, don't mind us while we set the table.

VALERIAN OLYMPOVICH (*to* OLYMP). Papa, I'm not marrying this ghastly peasant!

OLYMP VALERIANOVICH. She's not a ghastly peasant.

VALERIAN OLYMPOVICH. What do you mean? She's got the most peculiar smell.

OLYMP VALERIANOVICH. Don't be silly. She's probably just a bit nervous.

PAVEL SERGEEVICH (*to* VARVARA). How's Nastia?

VARVARA SERGEEVNA. She won't keep still and she's sneezing all over the place.

PAVEL SERGEEVICH. Typically selfish!

VALERIAN OLYMPOVICH (*to* OLYMP). But she's not educated, Papa. You can't make me marry her!

OLYMP VALERIANOVICH. Listen, in the old days we were rich and everybody was scared of us. And now we're still rich, so we're the ones who are terrified. Valerian, we need a Communist in the family. Her brother is a member of the Party. We need protecting. Think of him as a sort of insurance policy.

Enter a CARETAKER.

CARETAKER. Pavel Sergeevich, they want you at the house committee meeting.

PAVEL SERGEEVICH. A meeting? What's the meeting about?

CARETAKER. Rubbish.

PAVEL SERGEEVICH. Rubbish?

CARETAKER. Rubbish. Disposal of.

PAVEL SERGEEVICH. I've got my briefcase. Duty calls. All power to the Soviets.

PAVEL SERGEEVICH *exits with the* CARETAKER.

NADEJDA PETROVNA. Oh, what a pity! (*Indicating the portrait of Marx.*) Varvara, turn over that nasty foreigner. Do, please, everybody come and sit at the table. Olymp Valerianovich, please sit here.

The doorbell rings.

VARVARA SERGEEVNA. The doorbell! That must be the Communists.

EVERYONE. The Communists?

NADEJDA PETROVNA. They're early. Varvara, hide those vol-au-vents, and I'll go and I'll take a peek through the hole.

NADEJDA PETROVNA *exits.*

OLYMP VALERIANOVICH. Valerian!

VALERIAN OLYMPOVICH. Yes, Papa?

OLYMP VALERIANOVICH. Here, look at me. I don't look too respectable, do I?

VALERIAN OLYMPOVICH. No, Papa, you look like you always do.

Re-enter NADEJDA PETROVNA.

NADEJDA PETROVNA. Yes, it is the Communists. Varvara, turn over 'Copenhagen Twilight'.

VARVARA SERGEEVNA. Oh Mummy, I'm so nervous, I think I'm going to be sick.

The doorbell rings again.

NADEJDA PETROVNA. Good Heavens, they're ringing the bell again. Varvara, hurry! Hide those bottles, and I'll get the door. We're counting on you, God.

OLYMP VALERIANOVICH. Stop, Nadejda Petrovna, it's not properly proletarian for a lady to go to the door. You wait in the other room and I'll let them in with Valerian.

NADEJDA PETROVNA. God bless you, Olymp Valerianovich – if anything happens, call me. With God's help, dear Pavel will come back soon.

NADEJDA PETROVNA *and* VARVARA SERGEEVNA *exit. Enter the* ORGAN-GRINDER, *a* MAN *with a drum, and a* WOMAN *with a parrot and a tambourine.*

OLYMP VALERIANOVICH. This way, dear comrades, please come in.

MAN. Are these the Communists we're supposed to lie to about being their relatives?

ORGAN-GRINDER. Obviously, don't you see the medal?

VALERIAN OLYMPOVICH. Are these the Communists who promised to come?

OLYMP VALERIANOVICH. Oh, of course they are, look at the state of them. Sit down, comrades, please, do sit down. Pavel Sergeevich will be here shortly.

ORGAN-GRINDER. Pavel Sergeevich . . . For me, my dear citizen, he'll always be just my Pavlusha, tiny little Pavlushichenka.

Pause.

OLYMP VALERIANOVICH. Have you known Pavel Sergeevich for a long time, comrade?

ORGAN-GRINDER. How do you mean, know him, dear citizen? I'm his favourite uncle.

Pause. He sings.

VALERIAN OLYMPOVICH. Are you his actual uncle?

ORGAN-GRINDER. Right from the very moment he was born. I used to finish working at the factory and go straight to see him. There he'd be, in his mother's lap, sucking at her titty. So I do him horns with my fingers – just like this – and I'd ask him: 'Little Pavlushikoo, do you love the working class, then?' And, guess what? Quick as a flash he'd stop sucking and gurgle: 'I do love the working class, Uncle dear, I love the proletariat so much' – and then he'd go all happy and burp.

Pause.

WOMAN. And then, you know, he was such a *committed* little child, it's hard to credit.

OLYMP VALERIANOVICH. So you also knew him since childhood?

WOMAN. How could I not know him, sweetheart – I'm his favourite auntie.

MAN. Auntie. We are all aunties and uncles from the working class.

VALERIAN OLYMPOVICH (*aside*). My bride's family are a load of yobs.

WOMAN. I used to walk him by the factory and he'd grip that wall with his little fingers. And this is his brother.

MAN. His cousin, in actual point of fact, Mitia.

ORGAN-GRINDER. Our little Pavlushka.

OLYMP VALERIANOVICH. Excuse me, comrades, please. Valerian!

VALERIAN OLYMPOVICH. Yes, Papa . . .

OLYMP VALERIANOVICH (*to* VALERIAN). I'm surprised that Nadejda Petrovna didn't mention that these Communists were her relatives. Wherever has she got to? (*Aloud.*) All power to the Soviets!

VALERIAN OLYMPOVICH. Let's go, Papa.

OLYMP VALERIANOVICH *and* VALERIAN OLYMPOVICH *exit.*

WOMAN. Well, they seem to have swallowed that all right.

MAN. Now, let's drink.

Enter NADEJDA PETROVNA.

NADEJDA PETROVNA. Good evening, comrades.

ORGAN-GRINDER. Good evening, madam.

NADEJDA PETROVNA. Did you have a nice chat, comrades?

ORGAN-GRINDER. The conversation was enlightening, in fact it's made us all quite thirsty.

NADEJDA PETROVNA. I'll bring you some water in a moment, comrades.

ORGAN-GRINDER. What water? What do you mean – water? Is this some kind of joke, madam?

NADEJDA PETROVNA. Would I dare to joke with you, comrades?

ORGAN-GRINDER. Madam, let's proceed as agreed – first the vol-au-vents, then a bottle each.

NADEJDA PETROVNA. Comrades, whatever's the matter with you? We've never ever had vol-au-vents in the house, and as for wine, why, I don't even know what it looks like. I've heard about it, yes, but never actually seen any, so to speak.

ORGAN-GRINDER. What do you mean, you've never seen any?

Enter VARVARA SERGEEVNA.

VARVARA SERGEEVNA. Mummy, Tamara Leopoldovna is here!

NADEJDA PETROVNA. Tamara Leopoldovna? Heavens above, this'll be the end of me!

VARVARA SERGEEVNA. Please, everybody, please move into the next room. There's vodka next door.

The ORGAN-GRINDER *and his company exit.*

NADEJDA PETROVNA. Nastia, you idiot, get up from the chair immediately.

NASTIA. You can kill me if you like, but I won't stand up!

NADEJDA PETROVNA. Varvara, fetch me a bucket of water.

VARVARA SERGEEVNA *runs off.*

NASTIA. What do you want water for?

NADEJDA PETROVNA. We are going to wet the gun you're sitting on. Damp gunpowder doesn't explode, they say . . . Hurry up with the water!

Enter VARVARA SERGEEVNA *with buckets.*

Pour it under Nastia.

NASTIA. You'll drown me!

They pour the water under NASTIA.

NADEJDA PETROVNA. Now, get into the chest.

NASTIA. What do you mean, into the chest?

NADEJDA PETROVNA. Get in, I'm telling you.

NASTIA. But I'm all wet.

NADEJDA PETROVNA. You'll dry off in there.

NADEJDA PETROVNA *and* VARVARA SERGEEVNA *stuff* NASTIA *into the chest.*

Now, let in Tamara Leopoldovna, Varvara.

VARVARA SERGEEVNA *exits.*

And I'll lock the chest with a prayer for deliverance from the Anti-Christ.

Enter TAMARA LEOPOLDOVNA.

TAMARA LEOPOLDOVNA. I've been absolutely frantic with worry! Absolutely frantic! Tell me, quickly, say nothing bad has happened to it.

NADEJDA PETROVNA. It's been exceptionally well preserved, Tamara Leopoldovna.

TAMARA LEOPOLDOVNA. Oh, show it to me, Nadejda Petrovna.

NADEJDA PETROVNA. Don't you believe me, Tamara Leopoldovna?

TAMARA LEOPOLDOVNA. Oh, I'm so worried, Nadejda Petrovna.

NADEJDA PETROVNA. There are too many strangers lurking around, Tamara Leopoldovna, but, look, there's a bit of it sticking out.

TAMARA LEOPOLDOVNA. Oh, what a relief. I've been so worried, so dreadfully worried!

Enter IVAN IVANOVICH.

IVAN IVANOVICH. Militia, Militia!

NADEJDA PETROVNA. Why are you swearing in the dining room, Ivan Ivanovich? People have to eat in here, you know.

IVAN IVANOVICH. Your imprecations are of no avail, Nadejda Petrovna. The Militia will be here in a minute.

TAMARA LEOPOLDOVNA. Heavens above, the Militia!

Everyone but TAMARA LEOPOLDOVNA *runs off.* VALERIAN OLYMPOVICH *appears.*

VALERIAN OLYMPOVICH. What's up?

TAMARA LEOPOLDOVNA. Young man, do you believe in God?

VALERIAN OLYMPOVICH. Well, I do at home, but not at work.

TAMARA LEOPOLDOVNA. Then save a woman in direst need! Conceal my chest!

VALERIAN OLYMPOVICH. I beg your pardon? Oh! This chest! What's in it?

TAMARA LEOPOLDOVNA. Young man, I shall reveal to you a state secret. In this chest there's locked everything that's left of Russia in Russia.

VALERIAN OLYMPOVICH. Then it shouldn't weigh too much.

TAMARA LEOPOLDOVNA. I beg you, look after it, or everything is ruined.

VALERIAN OLYMPOVICH. All right, I'll try.

TAMARA LEOPOLDOVNA. If we can only get it to the taxi. (*Calls.*) Caretaker!

Enter the CARETAKER, *who, with* TAMARA
LEOPOLDOVNA *and* VALERIAN OLYMPOVICH,
carries away the chest.

Enter the MAN *with a drum, the* ORGAN-GRINDER, *the*
WOMAN *with the parrot and the tambourine,* NADEJDA
PETROVNA, IVAN IVANOVICH *and* OLYMP
VALERIANOVICH.

MAN. Who said the Militia were coming?

ORGAN-GRINDER. What's that about the Militia?

WOMAN. What Militia?

IVAN IVANOVICH. Aha! So are you afraid now, Nadejda
   Petrovna? You thought there was no law in the Soviet
   Republic . . . Well, there is, Nadejda Petrovna, there most
   certainly is. No state on earth would allow you to drown a
   citizen in noodles. Perhaps you surmise, Nadejda Petrovna,
   that as long as you pray with your gramophone that you're
   safe from the Law. Well, let me tell you that nowadays even
   a gramophone can be arrested for counter-revolutionary
   activities.

OLYMP VALERIANOVICH. Keep quiet about counter-
   revolutionary activities, comrade, her son is a Communist.

IVAN IVANOVICH. A Communist? Ha! I'd like to see him
   swear that on the Bible to the Militia!

OLYMP VALERIANOVICH. What does he mean, Nadejda
   Petrovna?

NADEJDA PETROVNA. Well, it seems he hasn't exactly
   joined fully . . . yet . . . but he's going to, Olymp
   Valerianovich.

OLYMP VALERIANOVICH. Hasn't joined yet? So you lied to
   me, Nadejda Petrovna? You're an agent provocateur.

IVAN IVANOVICH. Exactly, she's a provocateur.

OLYMP VALERIANOVICH. Now where's the dowry,
   Nadejda Petrovna?

ORGAN-GRINDER. Where's the booze, Nadejda Petrovna?

WOMAN. You are a liar, Nadejda Petrovna.

MAN. You are a schemer, Nadejda Petrovna.

IVAN IVANOVICH. You are a house-owner, Nadejda
Petrovna.

Enter VARVARA SERGEEVNA.

VARVARA SERGEEVNA. Oh my God, Ivan Ivanovich is
back! And if Pavel sees him, I shall die unknown and
untouched. I must get rid of him! Everybody dance!
Quickly, everybody, make noise! Lots of horrible nasty
noise. Look Mummy, we're driving him out. Play, go on,
play louder. Go on, dance, gentlemen.

Enter PAVEL SERGEEVICH.

PAVEL SERGEEVICH. Silence! I am a member of the Party!

IVAN IVANOVICH. Now, Pavel Sergeevich, you're not going
to scare me with that!

PAVEL SERGEEVICH. Oh no? Me and Molotov, we're like
that.

IVAN IVANOVICH. What sort of Communist are you, Pavel
Sergeevich? You don't even have papers. Communists
without papers don't exist.

PAVEL SERGEEVICH. You need papers? Papers?

IVAN IVANOVICH. You don't have any, do you, Pavel
Sergeevich? See! He doesn't have any papers!

PAVEL SERGEEVICH. Oh, don't I?

IVAN IVANOVICH. You don't have any!

PAVEL SERGEEVICH. Perhaps you'd like a quick glimpse of
my . . . mandate?

IVAN IVANOVICH. You don't have a mandate.

PAVEL SERGEEVICH. Oh, don't I? And what's this, then?

IVAN IVANOVICH (*reads*). 'Mandate.'

Everyone runs out, leaving the GULIACHKIN FAMILY *alone.*

PAVEL SERGEEVICH. Mummy, hold on to me or I'll arrest all Russia with this paper.

NADEJDA PETROVNA. Dear God in Heaven, they've stolen the chest!

PAVEL SERGEEVICH. The chest?

NADEJDA PETROVNA. The chest with the dress in, Pavel dear.

VARVARA SERGEEVNA. Don't forget that Nastia is still inside the dress, Mummy dear.

PAVEL SERGEEVICH. Why do you need the dress, Mummy, if I've got the mandate?

NADEJDA PETROVNA. Do you really have a mandate, Pavel?

PAVEL SERGEEVICH. Read it then, Mummy, if you don't believe me.

NADEJDA PETROVNA (*reads*). 'Man-date . . . '

PAVEL SERGEEVICH. Go on, Mummy, read on.

NADEJDA PETROVNA (*reads*). 'The following document is given to Pavel Sergeevich Guliachkin to affirm and testify that he is resident at Kirochny End, house number 13, flat number 6, confirmed forthwith by signature and stamp.'

PAVEL SERGEEVICH. Read on, Mummy.

NADEJDA PETROVNA. 'Signed by the chairman of the house committee, Commissar Pavel Sergeevich Guliachkin.'

PAVEL SERGEEVICH. A copy of this document has already been sent to the Kremlin, for the personal attention of Comrade Stalin.

End of Act Two.

ACT THREE

The apartment of OLYMP VALERIANOVICH SMETANICH.

His brother-in-law, AUTONOM SYGIZMUNDOVICH, *is searching through a pile of magazines.*

AUTONOM SYGIZMUNDOVICH. Agaphangel, where have you put the *Imperial Echo*?

Enter AGAPHANGEL.

AGAPHANGEL. I'm right here, Your Excellency.

AUTONOM SYGIZMUNDOVICH. What were you doing?

AGAPHANGEL. Excuse me, Your Excellency.

AUTONOM SYGIZMUNDOVICH. Excuse what?

AGAPHANGEL. I don't know, Your Excellency.

AUTONOM SYGIZMUNDOVICH. How do you mean, you don't know?

AGAPHANGEL. There's no way of telling, Your Excellency.

AUTONOM SYGIZMUNDOVICH. Where have you put the *Imperial Echo*?

AGAPHANGEL. It has vanished, Your Excellency

AUTONOM SYGIZMUNDOVICH. Vanished?

AGAPHANGEL. Without trace, Your Excellency. So completely that I can't find it anywhere.

AUTONOM SYGIZMUNDOVICH. Why ever not?

AGAPHANGEL. There's nothing left of it but a big hole, Your Excellency.

AUTONOM SYGIZMUNDOVICH. A hole?

AGAPHANGEL. A hole, Your Excellency.

AUTONOM SYGIZMUNDOVICH. How did that happen?

AGAPHANGEL. Nature called, Your Excellency.

AUTONOM SYGIZMUNDOVICH. What am I going to read now?

AGAPHANGEL. Permit me to make a suggestion, Your Excellency.

AUTONOM SYGIZMUNDOVICH. Permission granted.

AGAPHANGEL. Try the *International Illustrated* instead, Your Excellency, complete with photographs.

AUTONOM SYGIZMUNDOVICH. Let's see! What magnificent newspapers we used to have in the old days! (*Looks at a picture that falls out.*) What's this? His Imperial Majesty, Nicholas the Second! Stand to attention, man! Where did you find him?

AGAPHANGEL. In the toilet, Your Excellency.

AUTONOM SYGIZMUNDOVICH. Good God, did you find anybody else?

AGAPHANGEL. Well, yes, I did, Your Excellency.

AUTONOM SYGIZMUNDOVICH. Who?

AGAPHANGEL. King Albert of the Belgians, surrounded by his loyal subjects, in full colour, Your Excellency.

AUTONOM SYGIZMUNDOVICH. And where is he now?

AGAPHANGEL. Pardon me, Your Excellency. I wasn't paying attention and I'd already used him.

AUTONOM SYGIZMUNDOVICH. No wonder he's called the Martyr King. (*Goes through the pictures.*) 'His Imperial Majesty Nicholas the Second, Commander-in-Chief of the Armed Forces, tastes stew from a simple private's pot during enemy action.' Where are there heroes like that today? Just think what an example he was setting. Any minute His Imperial Majesty could have been blown sky high, but no, he didn't flinch and went on trying the stew under enemy fire. What do you say to that then, eh?

AGAPHANGEL. You're absolutely right, Your Excellency, he could easily have copped it – that army stew is worse than poison.

AUTONOM SYGIZMUNDOVICH. Nobody's looking, Agaphangel, let's hang this picture on the wall. Find some cardboard and mix up some glue this instant!

AGAPHANGEL. Certainly, Your Excellency,

AGAPHANGEL *goes.* ANATOLY, AUTONOM SYGIZMUNDOVICH*'s nephew, runs in.*

ANATOLY. The teacher's just told us some incredible news!

AUTONOM SYGIZMUNDOVICH. What news?

ANATOLY. It turns out there is no such thing as God.

AUTONOM SYGIZMUNDOVICH. Whatever do you mean?

ANATOLY. It's simple. God was a great big bourgeois con.

AUTONOM SYGIZMUNDOVICH. Then perhaps, young man, you will please tell me who has replaced him?

ANATOLY. Hydrogen.

AUTONOM SYGIZMUNDOVICH. What?

ANATOLY. Well, various gases actually.

AUTONOM SYGIZMUNDOVICH. Who told you that?

ANATOLY. At school. They gave us a special class with all sorts of weird diagrams. And it all proves that God has stopped.

AUTONOM SYGIZMUNDOVICH. Anatoly.

ANATOLY. Yes, Uncle?

AUTONOM SYGIZMUNDOVICH. You will not be going to school any more.

ANATOLY. No more school! Hurray!

AUTONOM SYGIZMUNDOVICH. You're not a child any more, Anatoly. It is time for you to become a man.

ANATOLY. What kind of man, Uncle?

AUTONOM SYGIZMUNDOVICH. What kind of man? Agaphangel!

Enter AGAPHANGEL.

AGPHANGEL. Yes, Your Excellency.

AUTONOM SYGIZMUNDOVICH. Unveil it now!

AGAPHANGEL *unveils a mannequin dressed in the full military regalia of a Tsarist General.*

That is the kind of man you will become.

ANATOLY. How can I manage that, Uncle?

AUTONOM SYGIZMUNDOVICH. I will train you, young man. Att-en-tion! You just wait. The old days will return.

ANATOLY. But Uncle, exactly when will the old days come back?

AUTONOM SYGIZMUNDOVICH. When will they come back to us? We have to go back to them.

ANATOLY. Then let's go as fast as possible, Uncle.

AUTONOM SYGIZMUNDOVICH. Left, right, left! Meanwhile, I'll just sit and rest a bit. I get so tired these days, you know. Agaphangel!

AGPHANGEL. Yes, Your Excellency.

AUTONOM SYGIZMUNDOVICH. Sing!

AGAPHANGEL *and* ANATOLY *march and sing.*

Enter VALERIAN OLYMPOVICH *and a* TAXI-DRIVER, *carrying the chest.*

VALERIAN OLYMPOVICH. Careful, careful. Put it down, put it down here. Right, thanks.

The TAXI-DRIVER *exits.*

There, Uncle, look! I've just saved Russia, all on my own.

AUTONOM SYGIZMUNDOVICH. What do you mean, saved Russia? What do you mean by that?

VALERIAN OLYMPOVICH. It's a state secret.

AUTONOM SYGIZMUNDOVICH. A state secret? What do you mean, a state secret?

VALERIAN OLYMPOVICH. It's in the chest, Uncle.

AUTONOM SYGIZMUNDOVICH. In the chest? What is in the chest?

VALERIAN OLYMPOVICH. This little chest contains all that is left in Russia of Russia.

AUTONOM SYGIZMUNDOVICH. What could be left of Russia? Even the *Imperial Echo* has become a hole.

ANATOLY. There's a hole in the chest as well.

AUTONOM SYGIZMUNDOVICH. Where's there a hole?

ANATOLY. I don't know where exactly, but it's leaking.

VALERIAN OLYMPOVICH. Leaking? Good God yes, it's leaking!

AUTONOM SYGIZMUNDOVICH. Well, that must mean that there's some sort of animal inside, or even a human being.

VALERIAN OLYMPOVICH. Uncle, what sort of animal or human being could be 'all that's left of Russia'?

AUTONOM SYGIZMUNDOVICH. What sort of animal or human being? Well, me, for example . . .

VALERIAN OLYMPOVICH. And what else?

AUTONOM SYGIZMUNDOVICH. And what else? Maybe there really is a human being inside. (*Speaks to the chest.*) Excuse me, do you happen to be a human being?

NASTIA (*out of the chest*). Certainly not, I'm a respectable young woman.

EVERYONE. A respectable young woman?!

VALERIAN OLYMPOVICH. Uncle, what respectable young woman could possibly be 'all that is left of Russia'?

AUTONOM SYGIZMUNDOVICH. A certain colonel – an old acquaintance of mine – once told me that he'd run into one of the Imperial Princesses on a beach in the Crimea.

VALERIAN OLYMPOVICH. Which one, Uncle?

AUTONOM SYGIZMUNDOVICH. Anastasia Nikolaevna. But I didn't believe him for an instant. The colonel was notoriously short-sighted and once even mistook himself for a general.

VALERIAN OLYMPOVICH. Anyway, Uncle, we should find out who she is. Excuse me, young lady, we're sorry to bother you, but could you possibly tell us your name?

NASTIA. Nastia.

VALERIAN OLYMPOVICH. What did you say?

NASTIA. Anastasia.

EVERYONE. It's her! It's her! It's her!

AUTONOM SYGIZMUNDOVICH. Lord above, it's her! Gentlemen, what are we going to do now?

VALERIAN OLYMPOVICH. Maybe it's another Anastasia. I'm going to ask her another question.

AUTONOM SYGIZMUNDOVICH. Ask her! But you have no right to directly address an Imperial Princess. The military code forbids it.

VALERIAN OLYMPOVICH. I'll ask her a question as if I don't suspect anything. By the way, madam, could you possibly tell us what your father happened to be called?

NASTIA. Nicholas!

AUTONOM SYGIZMUNDOVICH. Agaphangel!

AGAPHANGEL. Here, Your Excellency.

AUTONOM SYGIZMUNDOVICH. Hold me!

Enter OLYMP VALERIANOVICH.

OLYMP VALERIANOVICH. Gentlemen, I hear the Poles are up in arms against the Bolsheviks.

AUTONOM SYGIZMUNDOVICH. Never mind the Poles, there's going to be an uprising here!

OLYMP VALERIANOVICH. What are you talking about?

VALERIAN OLYMPOVICH. As a matter of fact, Papa, I have just saved Russia.

OLYMP VALERIANOVICH. How did you manage that?

VALERIAN OLYMPOVICH. It was quite simple really.

AUTONOM SYGIZMUNDOVICH. Olymp, he has rescued one of the Grand Duchesses!

OLYMP VALERIANOVICH. I don't believe you!

AUTONOM SYGIZMUNDOVICH. It's true, Olymp.

VALERIAN OLYMPOVICH. Anastasia Nikolaevna, Papa.

OLYMP VALERIANOVICH. Anastasia Nikolaevna? Impossible.

VALERIAN OLYMPOVICH. She told me so herself.

OLYMP VALERIANOVICH. Where is she, then?

AUTONOM SYGIZMUNDOVICH. In the chest. Olymp, right here!

OLYMP VALERIANOVICH. In the chest? Then we've got to liberate her. Gentlemen, we must organise a welcome party.

VALERIAN OLYMPOVICH *runs off and returns with a French baguette and salt.*

AUTONOM SYGIZMUNDOVICH. What are you going to do with that?

VALERIAN OLYMPOVICH. It's bread and salt for a patriotic welcome, Uncle. Dear Lord, what an historic moment! Just imagine, we are about to see our country's future in all its glory.

ANATOLY. Uncle, open the chest quickly, or all our country's future will leak away.

AUTONOM SYGIZMUNDOVICH. Are you ready, gentlemen?

EVERYONE. Ready.

AUTONOM SYGIZMUNDOVICH. Stand to attention, man! (*He opens the chest.*)

VALERIAN OLYMPOVICH. Uncle, do you know what you're opening?

AUTONOM SYGIZMUNDOVICH. Well, what am I opening?

VALERIAN OLYMPOVICH. A new page of history.

EVERYONE. Open it!

NASTIA (*climbs out*). Where am I?

AUTONOM SYGIZMUNDOVICH. Safe amongst your most loyal servants, Your Imperial Highness.

NASTIA. I think there's been some sort of mistake.

AUTONOM SYGIZMUNDOVICH. I'm ready to swear allegiance, Your Imperial Highness.

NASTIA. Oh, please don't go and do that!

OLYMP VALERIANOVICH. Believe us, Your Imperial Highness, had we but known, Your Imperial Highness, that all this time you were in Moscow . . .

NASTIA. Oh no, you've got it all mixed up! I just got here.

OLYMP VALERIANOVICH. All alone, Your Imperial Highness?

NASTIA. Now you're getting all confused.

OLYMP VALERIANOVICH. Pardon me, Your Imperial Highness. With whom then?

NASTIA. Don't be daft! With my uncle.

AUTONOM SYGIZMUNDOVICH. What! So the Grand Duke Mikhail Alexandrovich is also in Moscow. Hurrah!

EVERYONE. Hurrah!

NASTIA. Oh!

OLYMP VALERIANOVICH. Your Imperial Highness, what's the matter?

NASTIA. I'm all wet.

OLYMP VALERIANOVICH. We must get that dress off her at once or she'll catch a cold.

VALERIAN OLYMPOVICH. Papa, allow me.

AUTONOM SYGIZMUNDOVICH. You should be ashamed, Valerian, to speak of such things. You are no longer a child.

ANATOLY. Then please can I undress her, Uncle? I'm still a child.

AUTONOM SYGIZMUNDOVICH. That's enough of your indecency, young man. Don't forget – this is a question of saving Russia. I shall perform the delicate operation myself.

VALERIAN OLYMPOVICH. Excuse me, Uncle, I was the one who saved Russia first, so why should someone else get to undress her?

OLYMP VALERIANOVICH. Gentlemen, let's put Her Imperial Highness straight to bed.

Everyone, apart from OLYMP VALERIANOVICH, *lifts* NASTIA.

Just think! All Russia used to support people like that and now five of us can do it.

They carry her off. OLYMP VALERIANOVICH *picks up the phone, and dials furiously.*

If I hadn't seen her with my own eyes, I'd never have believed . . . Hello . . . hello . . . Stepan Stepanovich. Listen to me, Stepan Stepanovich, I have some astounding information from the surest of sources. Listen! Keep calm. Do exactly what I say. Just drop whatever you are doing and buy up as many of the old credit bonds . . . What? What? . . . Yes. The Tsar's, the Tsar's credit bonds . . . No, I am feeling perfectly well, thank you. I'm telling you, I have it from the most reliable . . . I can't go into that on the telephone. You know perfectly well that there's a commissar listening in on every line. Oh well, I'll tell you in Français, parce que les commissars Bolsheviques ne parle pas un word of it, ils ne sont que complete yobs anyway. Guess what? Quelle joyeux surprise! Le Grand Duchess Anastasia est arrivee ici à Moscow . . . what? Dans un big chest, do you understand, comprenez, Stepan, c'est notre big chance, au revoir Communism, eh? Les Bolsheviks will be dans le merde! Comprenez?! So, Stepan Stepanovich, achetez as many of the old bonds, comme vous pouvez, as you can, before you know who hears as they are going to soar demain. Didn't you learn any French at school? Idiot! Achetez très beaucoup et au revoir! (*He puts down the phone.*) An expensive education always comes in useful.

Enter AUTONOM SYGIZMUNDOVICH *and* VALERIAN OLYMPOVICH.

AUTONOM SYGIZMUNDOVICH. Quiet, gentlemen! Her Imperial Highness is fast asleep.

OLYMP VALERIANOVICH. Gentlemen, while Her Imperial Highness is sleeping, let's decide what we're going to do.

VALERIAN OLYMPOVICH. Well, for a start, Papa, I think we should keep our voices down.

OLYMP VALERIANOVICH. My God! If the Militia should find her! Valerian, you must marry Varvara Sergeevna today, immediately. We need a Communist in the family, urgently.

The telephone rings.

Who could that be? Hello? Oh, it's you, Ilyinkin. Quoi? Oui? Oui? Plus slowly, s'il vous plait. Oui. Au revoir le drapeau rouge! Oui, achetez stocks aussi, mais les old ones. Oui, je sais qu'ils ne sont worth a penny maintenant, mais tomorrow, get it, et Ilyinkin, pas un mot à anyone, c'est just between toi et moi, get it? Au revoir! Goodbye. (*He puts down the phone.*) All right, Valerian, get ready for the wedding and send for the Guliachkins immediately.

VALERIAN OLYMPOVICH *exits.*

AUTONOM SYGIZMUNDOVICH. You know, Olymp, I think it would more politic for Her Imperial Highness to assume an alias. Well, at least until we see how things pan out. It won't be easy getting her a housing permit. What if they work out who we've got staying here?

OLYMP VALERIANOVICH. Perhaps. It's bit dodgy, having a lodger called Romanov.

Enter NADEJDA PETROVNA.

NADEJDA PETROVNA. Olymp Valerianovich, in the name of God, don't believe him! That man is the incarnation of evil.

OLYMP VALERIANOVICH. What's wrong, Nadejda Petrovna?

AUTONOM SYGIZMUNDOVICH. Who is the incarnation of evil?

NADEJDA PETROVNA. Ivan Ivanovich.

OLYMP VALERIANOVICH. Which Ivan Ivanovich?

NADEJDA PETROVNA. Ivan Ivanovich Shironkin, our lodger.

AUTONOM SYGIZMUNDOVICH. What about him?

NADEJDA PETROVNA. 'Nadejda Petrovna,' he says, 'I know that your son is no Communist because he is descended from parasites.' I tell you, Olymp Valerianovich, I've lived with my one-hundred-per-cent-legitimate husband for nineteen long years and that, that heretic, says my beautiful son is descended from parasites.

OLYMP VALERIANOVICH. But Nadejda Petrovna, who does he think could be such a fool, excuse my language, to believe rubbish like that?

NADEJDA PETROVNA. You, Olymp Valerianovich! You! Only don't believe him. In the name of God, Olymp Valerianovich, don't believe him.

OLYMP VALERIANOVICH. I won't even listen to him, Nadejda Petrovna.

NADEJDA PETROVNA. Olymp Valerianovich, who could possibly think that my sweet little Pavel isn't a Communist when you yourself, Olymp Valerianovich, saw that he has a genuine mandate? Why, it's so genuine I can hardly sleep at nights. What if he were to arrest me?

AUTONOM SYGIZMUNDOVICH. Why ever would he arrest his own mother?

NADEJDA PETROVNA. Oh, you can't imagine how the idea has possessed him, Olymp Valerianovich. It's like he's on a drinking binge. He must have got that from his father. When his daddy used to drink, he'd roll up his sleeves and say: 'Let me at them!'

OLYMP VALERIANOVICH. At whom?

NADEJDA PETROVNA. At the Germans. 'Kill the Krauts!' he used to roar, 'or I'll make them all Orthodox!' He had a terrible temper.

OLYMP VALERIANOVICH. Is your son that fierce?

NADEJDA PETROVNA. But he's a little lamb with his betters, Olymp Valerianovich!

OLYMP VALERIANOVICH. Nadejda Petrovna, let's have the wedding now!

NADEJDA PETROVNA. Oh, Olymp Valerianovich, you mean you've made up your mind?

OLYMP VALERIANOVICH. Today, Nadejda Petrovna! Let's have the wedding today! I've only one tiny condition.

NADEJDA PETROVNA. A condition, Olymp Valerianovich?

OLYMP VALERIANOVICH. Nadejda Petrovna, I want your son to move in with us as well.

NADEJDA PETROVNA. Oh, don't worry about that, Olymp Valerianovich, my entire family is moving in.

OLYMP VALERIANOVICH. What? Don't frighten me like that. No, Nadejda Petrovna, why would you all need to move in with us?

NADEJDA PETROVNA. Don't you worry about a thing, Olymp Valerinovich. It's no trouble at all. We'll just pack up our things and come straight away.

OLYMP VALERIANOVICH. Just make sure, Nadejda Petrovna, that he doesn't forget his mandate.

NADEJDA PETROVNA. Oh, Olymp Valerianovich, he wouldn't move an inch without his mandate. Him and his mandate, they're stitched together. Why, only this morning he went to the baths and all the time he had his soap in his right hand and his mandate in his left. Getting soggy all the time. 'Let them never forget,' he said, 'that I'm a big cheese even when I'm in the rude.'

OLYMP VALERIANOVICH. So then, I'll be expecting you, Nadejda Petrovna.

NADEJDA PETROVNA. Back in a jiffy, dear Olymp Valerianovich!

She goes. The telephone rings. AUTONOM SYGIZ-MUNDOVICH *answers.*

OLYMP VALERIANOVICH. Who is it now, Autonom?

AUTONOM SYGIZMUNDOVICH. It's Zarkhin, Olymp.

OLYMP VALERIANOVICH. Good God! What does he want?

AUTONOM SYGIZMUNDOVICH. He wants you to buy stocks, Olymp.

OLYMP VALERIANOVICH. What stocks?

AUTONOM SYGIZMUNDOVICH. What stocks, he's asking? Pre-1917 ones? He says old stocks, Olymp. Yes, yes. I hear you. Olymp, he says . . . who's appeared? Who? Who's in Moscow? The Grand Duke Mikhailovich is already in Moscow?! Good Heavens! What? What? Olymp! And apparently Her Imperial Highness Anastasia Nikolaevna is hiding somewhere in Moscow! Of course. Of course. Don't you worry. (*He puts down the phone. To* OLYMP.) Olymp. He makes you promise on your word of honour not to tell a soul.

OLYMP VALERIANOVICH. Well, that's it! If Zarkhin believes it, it must be true.

They leave. Enter IVAN IVANOVICH.

IVAN IVANOVICH (*aside*). What a pity I didn't go to university. It would have made talking to Olymp Valerianovich a lot easier.

Enter NASTIA, *wearing only a sheet.*

What a vision!

NASTIA. Where's that dress gone to?

IVAN IVANOVICH. Naked as a nymph, beshrouded in a sheet. How can I control myself?

NASTIA. Oh, don't you look, now!

IVAN IVANOVICH. Excuse my impertinence, madam, but you don't seem to be wearing any clothes.

NASTIA. Oh, I thought it was some man or other, but it's only you, Ivan Ivanovich!

IVAN IVANOVICH. Anastasia Nikolaevna? What are you doing here?

NASTIA. Actually, Ivan Ivanovich, I don't know where I am.

IVAN IVANOVICH. How do you mean, you don't know where you are, Anastasia Nikolaevna? You're lounging around without a stitch on.

NASTIA. It's not my fault, Ivan Ivanovich, my dress just dissolved.

IVAN IVANOVICH. Dissolved?

NASTIA. You probably won't believe me, but I've been drowned.

IVAN IVANOVICH. Drowned? Where did you drown?

NASTIA. On the chair.

IVAN IVANOVICH. Anastasia Nikolaevna, you must think I'm a compete idiot.

NASTIA. Honestly, Ivan Ivanovich, I'm in what you might call a desperate plight, and all you can do is stand there and cast aspersions.

IVAN IVANOVICH. Forgive me, Anastasia Nikolaevna, but how did you manage to get here?

NASTIA. In this chest.

IVAN IVANOVICH. I don't think I'm quite following, Anastasia Nikolaevna. Perhaps you'd better tell me the whole story right from the very beginning.

NASTIA. Well, all right then, Ivan Ivanovich, the whole story right from the very beginning. First of all, they made me wear a really posh dress, then they wet me all over, and then they put me into this chest and then they carried me here.

IVAN IVANOVICH. I'm afraid, Anastasia Nikolaevna, that I am still somewhat confused. And what did they do to you when they finally got you here?

NASTIA. Well, they took all my clothes off and put me in a bed.

IVAN IVANOVICH. At last, Anastasia Nikolaevna, I understand it all. You have been sold into Sodom.

NASTIA. What's that you said?

IVAN IVANOVICH. It is all hideously clear!

NASTIA. How awful! Sodom.

IVAN IVANOVICH. And what is worse, Anastasia Nikolaevna, your employer, Nadejda Petrovna, is a trafficker in human flesh.

NASTIA. The things that people get up to! And she looked such a nice person.

IVAN IVANOVICH. Why else should she pack innocent young women into chests and send them to strange men?

NASTIA. Oh, Ivan Ivanovich, what do you think they're going to do to me?

IVAN IVANOVICH. It seems abundantly clear, Anastasia Nikolaevna, Olymp Valerianovich is going to make you his concubine.

NASTIA. Make me his what?

IVAN IVANOVICH. His concubine.

NASTIA. What's that then?

IVAN IVANOVICH. A concubine, Anastasia Nikolaevna, is a sort of cook, who gives illegitimate pleasure to men.

NASTIA. Oh my God! What an awful thing to do to an unmarried young lady! But, on the other hand, Ivan Ivanovich, maybe he's like that bloke in *Sold into Lust*?

IVAN IVANOVICH. Who in *Sold into Lust*?

NASTIA. Well, that large young baron with cruel eyes that kidnaps an obscure but virtuous serving-wench and carries her off to a Catholic church where he marries her because of his irrepressible love.

IVAN IVANOVICH. In a Communist state, Anastasia Nikolaevna, there is no love, only gender-related issues. And, anyway, why would Olymp Valerianovich marry someone like you when he's rotten with money? They took me in, too – I thought that Olymp Valerianovich was going to rip Pavel Sergeevich apart, but now I see that they are all in it together.

NASTIA. So whatever can I do, Ivan Ivanovich?

IVAN IVANOVICH. What can you do, Anastasia Nikolaevna? You are a fallen woman.

NASTIA. Oh, Ivan Ivanovich, you're educated, surely you can think of something.

IVAN IVANOVICH (*kneels and kisses* NASTIA*'s hand*). I kneel not to you, Anastasia Nikolaevna, but to your Great Suffering. (*Stands.*) Bye bye now, must dash.

NASTIA. Hang on, Ivan Ivanovich, I'm coming, too.

IVAN IVANOVICH. Where do you think you're off to like that? You'll be reported to the Militia for using the public thoroughfare as a bath-house.

NASTIA. Please, Ivan Ivanovich, I beg you. Don't leave me here!

IVAN IVANOVICH. Here? Whatever are you saying, Anastasia Nikolaevna? If Olymp Valerianovich finds us in such a compromising situation, I shall be leaving by the window and not the lift. (*He hears steps.*) That's it! I'm done for now!

IVAN IVANOVICH *hides under her sheet.*

Enter AGAPHANGEL *with the dress,* OLYMP VALERIANOVICH, AUTONOM SYGIZMUNDOVICH *and* VALERIAN OLYMPOVICH.

AGAPHANGEL. The dress is quite dry now.

AUTONOM SYGIZMUNDOVICH. Are you sure it's dry?

AGAPHANGEL. It's dry, Your Excellency, dry as a bone.

OLYMP VALERIANOVICH. It's dry, Autonom, dry as a bone.

NASTIA. Please don't come in, there's a young lady in here with nothing on.

OLYMP VALERIANOVICH. Pardon me, Your Most Imperial Highness, but are you still in bed or would you like me to help you get dressed?

IVAN IVANOVICH (*aside, to* NASTIA, *hiding*). I knew it, you're going to be his concubine.

NASTIA (*aside*). I think things are going to get sticky.

AUTONOM SYGIZMUNDOVICH. Would you care to wash yourself, Your Imperial Highness? Here's a basin.

IVAN IVANOVICH (*aside*). A basin? I thought as much, here we go!

NASTIA. Kill me rather, but I will not be dishonoured!

VALERIAN OLYMPOVICH. I beg you to forgive me, Your Imperial Highness, if in any way it appeared that I . . . it was a most unfortunate misunderstanding if . . .

NASTIA. Don't you go thinking you can trick me with all those fancy words, you . . . I know what you're after and I'm off . . .

OLYMP VALERIANOVICH. How can you mistrust him, Your Imperial Highness? Here beats a true Russian soul! How can you doubt his passionate attachment and deep love?

NASTIA. Love? Really? You're having me on.

OLYMP VALERIANOVICH. I swear to you, Your Imperial Highness.

VALERIAN OLYMPOVICH. Do not leave us, Your Imperial Highness.

NASTIA. I'd better go . . .

VALERIAN OLYMPOVICH. We beg you, Your Imperial Highness, do not leave us! Stay here! Only change your name!

NASTIA. Are you having me on?

VALERIAN OLYMPOVICH. No, I swear, Your Imperial Highness.

NASTIA (*aside*). What did I tell you, Ivan Ivanovich, it is just like in *Sold into Lust*. (*Aloud.*) Very well, my dearest darling, no longer shall I let you suffer, I shall accept your hand. Pray, hand me my garments. After we are married, will you call me Nastia?

VALERIAN OLYMPOVICH. Papa, I've suddenly gone all peculiar!

IVAN IVANOVICH (*aside*). Don't trust them!

AUTONOM SYGIZMUNDOVICH. Answer her, Valerian!

VALERIAN OLYMPOVICH. I can't, Uncle, my head is spinning!

IVAN IVANOVICH (*aside*). See! He's changed his mind!

OLYMP VALERIANOVICH. Your Imperial Highness, could my son possibly dream of such an honour as to marry you?

NASTIA (*aside*). See! They're not nasty people! (*Aloud.*) Certainly, thus do I cast aside the sham veil of pretence.

OLYMP VALERIANOVICH. When would you like the ceremony, Your Imperial Highness?

NASTIA. Why not this afternoon? I am free of all engagements!

IVAN IVANOVICH (*aside*). They are counter-revolutionary perverts, and are leading us into a trap!

OLYMP VALERIANOVICH. What was that?

NASTIA. Oh, nothing! I was just talking to myself. And if you think my voice sounds a bit mannish, it's on account of my cold, which is something shocking.

OLYMP VALERIANOVICH. Of course, Your Imperial Highness.

IVAN IVANOVICH (*aside*). How am I going to get out of here?

NASTIA. Pray, gentlemen, hand me my garments.

AGAPHANGEL. Here is your dress, Your Imperial Highness.

NASTIA. Please be so good as to shut your eyes, as I get dressed. (*Aside.*) Get in that chest, Ivan Ivanovich, and keep your trap shut! (*Aloud.*) Open wide, gentlemen! I have changed my mind on a mere whim, and shall get dressed in the adjoining chamber. Just a sec.

NASTIA *exits to get dressed.*

AUTONOM SYGIZMUNDOVICH. Agaphangel!

AGAPHANGEL. Yes, Your Excellency?

AUTONOM SYGIZMUNDOVICH. Quick. Take a look in the lavatory and make sure Her Imperial Highness doesn't meet any of her relatives in there.

Enter ANATOLY.

ANATOLY. Papa, the wedding carriage is ready.

OLYMP VALERIANOVICH. What wedding carriage?

ANATOLY. The one you booked to take Valerian and Varvara Sergeevna to the Register Office.

OLYMP VALERIANOVICH. What – Varvara Sergeevna?

AUTONOM SYGIZMUNDOVICH. Dear oh dear! They'll be here any minute!

OLYMP VALERIANOVICH. What are we going to do, Valerian?

VALERIAN OLYMPOVICH. Papa, I don't know, my head is spinning . . .

OLYMP VALERIANOVICH. Autonom, listen, do me a favour, explain to them, diplomatically, that you're very sorry but the wedding's off.

AUTONOM SYGIZMUNDOVICH. Diplomatically? I'll try, Olymp, I'll try. But just think, Olymp, what an extraordinary situation: at this very moment in history, this young woman represents the future of all Russia, and our Valerian is going to marry her!

OLYMP VALERIANOVICH. Exactly, Autonom! And what's more, that means that our Valerian, so to speak, is going to be one half of the entirety of all Russia! What a responsibility!

AUTONOM SYGIZMUNDOVICH. Now that's what I call a dowry! What's up with you, Valerian?

VALERIAN OLYMPOVICH. Uncle, my head is spinning . . .

Enter NASTIA.

NASTIA. Here I am, gentlemen, completely dressed and wearing my shoes as well.

OLYMP VALERIANOVICH. Your Imperial Highness, the carriage awaits.

NASTIA. A carriage! Oh, lovely, let's go, let's go!

NASTIA, OLYMP VALERIANOVICH *and* VALERIAN OLYMPOVICH *exit.*

AUTONOM SYGIZMUNDOVICH. So, Anatoly, how will it feel to be the brother-in-law of Her Imperial Highness?

ANATOLY. If only Mummy had survived, Uncle, she'd be so happy.

Enter AGAPHANGEL *with glue.*

AUTONOM SYGIZMUNDOVICH. What's that you have there?

AGAPHANGEL. The glue, your Excellency.

AUTONOM SYGIZMUNDOVICH. What glue? Oh yes. Anatoly!

ANATOLY. Yes, Uncle.

AUTONOM SYGIZMUNDOVICH. We need to glue this picture onto some cardboard.

ANATOLY. Isn't that the papa of the woman in the chest, Uncle?

AUTONOM SYGIZMUNDOVICH. Yes, Anatoly, he is the Sovereign of all Russia.

ANATOLY. Right, I've glued him, Uncle, what do you want me to stick him on to?

AUTONOM SYGIZMUNDOVICH. Agaphangel, you've forgotten the cardboard.

AGAPHANGEL *exits.*

ANATOLY. Where do you want me to put him, Uncle?

AUTONOM SYGIZMUNDOVICH. Put him on the chair for the time being.

ANATOLY *puts Nicholas's portrait on the chair, with the glued side facing up. Enter* NADEJDA PETROVNA *with the gramophone,* VARVARA SERGEEVNA *in a wedding dress, and* PAVEL SERGEEVICH *with a briefcase.*

NADEJDA PETROVNA. Thanks be to God, at last we're moving in to your flat, Autonom Sygizmundovich!

AUTONOM SYGIZMUNDOVICH. What a rabble! How can I get rid of them diplomatically?

NADEJDA PETROVNA. Dear Autonom Sygizmundovich, permit me to introduce my children.

AUTONOM SYGIZMUNDOVICH. I'm really sorry, Nadejda Petrovna, but it's not my fault, believe me . . .

NADEJDA PETROVNA. And where is the bridegroom, Autonom Sygizmundovich?

VARVARA SERGEEVNA. Oh! Don't say such naughty words, Mummy, you're embarrassing me!

AUTONOM SYGIZMUNDOVICH. I couldn't agree with you more, young lady, it's better not to talk about it.

ANATOLY. If it's my brother Valerian you mean, Papa has just taken him to church to get married.

NADEJDA PETROVNA. Heavens above! We stand here blabbing all sorts of nonsense while they're waiting for us in the church! Pavel, do something to Varvara's nose, more powder! Let's go, Autonom Sygizmundovich, we're dreadfully late!

AUTONOM SYGIZMUNDOVICH. You see, Nadejda Petrovna, I must explain to you . . . how can I phrase this diplomatically . . . there's going to be no wedding.

PAVEL SERGEEVICH. What do you mean, no wedding?

AUTONOM SYGIZMUNDOVICH. Absolutely no wedding.

VARVARA SERGEEVNA. Mummy, I think I've just been humiliated.

NADEJDA PETROVNA. What do you mean, absolutely no wedding? Why absolutely no wedding?

AUTONOM SYGIZMUNDOVICH. I am not at liberty to say.

NADEJDA PETROVNA. God Almighty, what's going on? We've been humiliated, just like that – humiliated. What have we done to make Valerian Olympovich hate us? My daughter is a polished young lady and has nothing to be ashamed of. Perhaps he thinks our dear Varvara's got a peculiar nose. Well, let me tell you, our Varvara will make a wonderful wife whatever her nose is like.

AUTONOM SYGIZMUNDOVICH. It isn't about her nose, Nadejda Petrovna, it's about something deeper . . .

VARVARA SERGEEVNA. But I am very deep, Autonom Sygizmundovich . . .

AUTONOM SYGIZMUNDOVICH. Of course you are, Varvara Sergeevna, but it isn't your fault. Do please, I beg you, try not to take this personally.

NADEJDA PETROVNA. Well, then, Autonom Sygizmundovich, whose fault is it? It's me, isn't it, Autonom Sygizmundovich?

Just tell me, I knew it all along. I'm the problem. It's all about me. Well, forget me, I'm nothing – just the mother, just a tiny little bit of useless, filthy, worthless rubbish, Autonom Sygizmundovich.

AUTONOM SYGIZMUNDOVICH. I entirely agree with you, Nadejda Petrovna, but . . .

NADEJDA PETROVNA. If I were Valerian Olympovich, I'd just spit in my miserable little face and completely ignore me . . .

AUTONOM SYGIZMUNDOVICH. You are absolutely right, Nadejda Petrovna, but there's another reason.

NADEJDA PETROVNA. What *is* the reason, then?

AUTONOM SYGIZMUNDOVICH. That is a secret, Nadejda Petrovna, and I am not at liberty to explain.

NADEJDA PETROVNA. Not at liberty! Pavel dear, you're a celebrity now – can you get some sense out of him, please?

PAVEL SERGEEVICH. You seem to have been leading us up the garden path, my man. Why will there be no wedding?

AUTONOM SYGIZMUNDOVICH. How dare you talk to me like this?

PAVEL SERGEEVICH. How dare I? Don't you know who I am? I am on first-name terms with the Third International himself!

AUTONOM SYGIZMUNDOVICH. I'm ruined! They are going to arrest me.

PAVEL SERGEEVICH. How dare I? I was an undercover agent during the October Revolution!

AUTONOM SYGIZMUNDOVICH. They'll shoot me, no doubt about it.

PAVEL SERGEEVICH. I even happen to be Chairman . . . of the housing committee. An Official!

AUTONOM SYGIZMUNDOVICH. Forgive me, comrade, but I'm . . .

PAVEL SERGEEVICH. Silence! I am a member of the Party!

ANATOLY. Silence! I am the brother-in-law of Her Imperial Highness, the Grand Duchess Anastasia Nikolaevna!

PAVEL SERGEEVICH collapses on the chair, terrified. Enter STEPAN STEPANOVICH and his wife, FELIZIATA GORDEEVNA with flowers.

FELIZIATA GORDEEVNA. Christ is risen, Autonom Sygizmundovich! Please let me kiss you, it feels like it's Easter already!

STEPAN STEPANOVICH. Forgive me for omitting the usual social niceties, but the future of Holy Russia is at stake.

Enter ILYINKIN with his wife, ILYINKINA.

ILYINKIN. Gentlemen, for God's sake, tell us, is Grand Duke Mikhail Alexandrovich in the bag or not?

FELIZIATA GORDEEVNA. Really, how could you ask questions like that so indelicately?

Enter ZARKHIN, his wife, ARIADNA PAVLINOVNA ZARKHINA, and the young Zarkhin daughters, TOSIA and SIUSIA.

ARIADNA PAVLINOVNA. Honestly, those Bolsheviks are so impudent, I was walking with my husband in the street just now, and a militiaman was standing on the corner, whistling away, pretending that nothing had happened.

Enter KRANTIC NARKIS SMARAGDOVICH with a camera.

NARKIS SMARAGDOVICH. Tell me, which way round is more elegant?

ZARKHIN. What are you talking about?

NARKIS SMARAGDOVICH. I only wanted to capture . . .

STEPAN STEPANOVICH. To capture what?

NARKIS SMARAGDOVICH. The Renaissance.

ILYINKIN. What Renaissance?

NARKIS SMARAGDOVICH. The resurrection . . . of our long-suffering Motherland . . . the rebirth of Tsarist Russia. And since this event is bound to stir the entire world, I felt a little photo-opportunity was called for. Having heard that Her Imperial Highness has honoured us with . . .

PAVEL SERGEEVICH. What Imperial Highness?

NARKIS SMARAGDOVICH. Calm down, I'm taking a photo.

AUTONOM SYGIZMUNDOVICH. Hold him! Hold him! Agaphangel!

Enter AGAPHANGEL.

AGAPHANGEL. Here, Your Excellency.

AUTONOM SYGIZMUNDOVICH. Quick. Lock the doors and keep them covered.

AGAPHANGEL *stands by the door with the gun.*

EVERYONE. What's up? What's wrong? What's that?

AUTONOM SYGIZMUNDOVICH. Gentlemen, we've been overheard.

ARIADNA PAVLINOVNA. Who's overheard us?

AUTONOM SYGIZMUNDOVICH. The Communists.

EVERYONE. Communists!

FELIZIATA GORDEEVNA. Run for your lives!

They all rush to the exit.

AGAPHANGEL. Stop, or I'll shoot! I'll shoot you all!

STEPAN STEPANOVICH. Help! We're surrounded.

NARKIS SMARAGDOVICH. I think there's only one of them.

They turn to PAVEL SERGEEVICH.

NADEJDA PETROVNA. Good people, spare my son – he's a devout Christian, really! Autonom Sygizmundovich, I tell you, he's only a Communist looked at one way, from the other side he's . . .

PAVEL SERGEEVICH. From the other side, I'm nothing of the sort!

He stands up and bows. Nicholas II's portrait is glued to his backside.

ZARKHIN. We should try and find out his real identity.

TOSIA. But Papa, he's got two.

ZARKHIN. What do you mean – two?

TOSIA. I'm really rather embarrassed to mention it in company, Papa, but he does seem to have some sort of identity on his . . . rude part.

EVERYONE. Where?

TOSIA. There.

AUTONOM SYGIZMUNDOVICH. Go on, bend over, young man. Good Heavens! Everyone, attention!

PAVEL SERGEEVICH. Who is it, Mummy, me?

AUTONOM SYGIZMUNDOVICH. No, young man, it's us.

ANATOLY. Gentlemen, they're coming, they're coming!

AGAPHANGEL. Your Excellency, they'll be here any minute!

EVERYONE. They are coming, coming. Stand in a line, gentlemen. Hush, they are coming.

Enter NASTIA, OLYMP VALERIANOVICH *and* VALERIAN OLYMPOVICH.

AUTONOM SYGIZMUNDOVICH. Music, everyone! Hurrah! Hurrah! Hurrah!

EVERYONE. Hurrah!

AUTONOM SYGIZMUNDOVICH. Dear ladies and gentlemen, Her Imperial Highness is touched by your loyal welcome. Dear ladies and gentlemen . . .

OLYMP VALERIANOVICH. Your Imperial Highness . . .

AUTONOM SYGIZMUNDOVICH. Oh, do shut up, Olymp, I haven't finished yet!

OLYMP VALERIANOVICH. Shut up?! I've been shut up for seven years! Your Imperial Highness, for seven long years we have yearned for this day, and now, it has arrived. May I be permitted, Your Imperial Highness, to say a few words?

NASTIA. Pray continue.

OLYMP VALERIANOVICH. For seven years, Your Imperial Highness, for seven years the Bolsheviks have been pouring refuse on our heads . . . and each of those years seems like a decade, or even a century. For seven hundred years they have been drowning us in excrement, Your Imperial Highness.

EVERYONE. Drowning us in excrement, Your Imperial Highness!

OLYMP VALERIANOVICH. Even while the gallant White Army was spilling its young blood into the flowing wounds of our suffering Motherland, even during all that noble spilling and flowing, the Bolsheviks never left off shitting on us. Not once, did they let up. 'You prey on the people,' they said. 'You bully the people,' they said. 'You shoot the people,' they said. Now I stand before almighty Russia herself, and look Russia herself straight in the eye, and I say to her, nay I shout: 'You show me that man that I've shot! Let him come here and accuse me!' But he won't, will he? Because no such person has ever existed!

EVERYONE. Bravo! Bravo!

OLYMP VALERIANOVICH. Your Imperial Highness, I open my heart to you and here I am, standing in front of you completely naked, so to speak.

SIUSIA. Papa, I can't see!

OLYMP VALERIANOVICH. What I say is this, Your Imperial Highness. Yes. Yes, we loved the people. And oh, Your Imperial Highness, how we loved them. Take me, for example, I've dedicated my whole life to the working people, I have. Before 1917, I had a factory and there were five hundred of them working in it, people that is. And, dear God, I loved those people. And then they took the people away from me. I'm ready to die for the people, Your Imperial Highness, because I can't live without them. Your Imperial Highness, give us back our people.

EVERYONE. Give us back our people!

OLYMP VALERIANOVICH. Yes, Your Imperial Highness, we loved the people. But we also loved the land. How could those Bolsheviks love them? How could they love the people or the land? They never had any! But I, Your Imperial Highness, I had land. Quite a lot of land, actually, two thousand nine hundred and thirty-three acres of land, and they took it away from me, my land, the land of our fathers, the land of our mothers.

EVERYONE. Give us back our mothers!

OLYMP VALERIANOVICH. But most of all we loved Russia. And what do we see now? – She's vanished. She's been changed, she's been pulled out from under our feet, and here we are, hanging in the air, Your Imperial Highness. I'm hanging in the air, completely weightless. Yes, Your Imperial Highness, they sucked all the weight out of us and we're just left hanging in the air. And way down below our feet there's no Russia, just thousands and thousands of miles of vast, empty nothing . . . . What if we fall, Your Imperial Highness? Our legs are dangling above an enormous hole and we don't even have somewhere to fall on! But I have always believed, it is my deep belief, Your Imperial Highness, that a new Columbus will appear and discover Russia. And he has appeared, this Columbus, and this Columbus is none other than you, Your Imperial Highness! The waves may lash, the winds may roar, but our ship is on the right track. Already we can hear from the tall tops'l, or mizzen, or whatever, that joyful cry of 'Land ahoy!' or to be precise: 'Two thousand nine hundred and thirty-three acres ahoy!'

EVERYONE. Give us back our two thousand nine hundred and thirty-three acres, Your Imperial Majesty!

NASTIA. Wow, now this is what I call a proper wedding!

EVERYONE. Hurrah!

A 'Hurrah' is heard outside. As the 'Hurrah' fades, a long moan is heard.

VOICES. Did you hear that? What was that? What's that?

OLYMP VALERIANOVICH. Gentlemen, gentlemen, could it be the people's cry of happiness!

ARIADNA PAVLINOVNA. Do the people know already?

OLYMP VALERIANOVICH. Of course they do. Why else would they shout 'Hurrah'?

ZARKHIN. Are you sure that was a 'Hurrah'?

OLYMP VALERIANOVICH. I heard it clearly.

STEPAN STEPANOVICH. It means that the people support us. Hurrah!

EVERYONE. Hurrah!

OLYMP VALERIANOVICH. Ssshhh! Listen!

IVAN IVANOVICH (*from within the chest*). Help!

ZARKHIN. Do you hear it?

AUTONOM SYGIZMUNDOVICH. No. Do you?

ZARKHIN. Me neither.

STEPAN STEPANOVICH. Let's try listening again.

OLYMP VALERIANOVICH. Listen.

AUTONOM SYGIZMUNDOVICH. The people are silent.

PAVEL SERGEEVICH. Women and men and even little
children, listen to me! You see before you a hero ready to
lay down his life for the revolution! Women and men and
even little children, this slut is planning to seize the Russian
throne, but she will sit on it only over my cold body. I am
absolutely serious.

STEPAN STEPANOVICH. What is he saying? He's a
madman! Your Imperial Highness, he's gone berserk!

PAVEL SERGEEVICH. Comrades! Was our struggle in vain?
Why did we die as martyrs in the red field of battle, we –
workers from field and plough and chairmen of housing
committees? Women and men and even little children,
I refuse, I absolutely refuse, as any Bolshevik hero, would,
to swear allegiance to this counter-revolution of generals,
popes and flat-owners.

ILYINKINA. For God's sake, can't someone shut him up!?

PAVEL SERGEEVICH. Comrades! No one can silence me.
We will all always, as one man, speak out against generals,
popes and flat-owners, because this is what our great idea is
all about, our sacred obsession. Women and men and even
little children, you will never manage to strangle the spark
of revolution while we exist . . . me and my mother, that is.
And do not think for one moment that I am only afraid of
her. Nothing of the sort. Let's go to England, I wouldn't
even be afraid of the Queen of England herself. You watch
me, I can tick off the Tsar himself. You think that they can
escape my vengeance by fleeing to distant climes. I swear to
you, comrades, distance will not defeat me. Oh no. I'll tell
all the Tsars, all – the English one, the Italian one, the
Turkish one and the French one. Tsars, do you hear me? –
(*Aside.*) Mummy, what's going to happen now? (*Aloud.*)
Tsars . . . you are all complete and total bastards!

VOICES. Arrest him! Arrest him!

ILYINKIN. Gentlemen, it's a conspiracy, arrest him,
somebody!

NADEJDA PETROVNA. You keep your hands off my son, he's just a little tipsy.

PAVEL SERGEEVICH. Tipsy? Who is tipsy? Me tipsy? Smell my breath, see! Not a whiff! That's really important, comrades, you must remember that I was absolutely sober. The crucial thing is that I made my Great Declaration whilst completely sober. And I'd like you to write down the following words – have you got a pen? – because these words will probably promote me for life. Please listen carefully, Your Imperial Highness! You are . . . a silly cow!

EVERYONE. O-h-h-h-h!!!

AUTONOM SYGIZMUNDOVICH. Soldiers!

AGAPHANGEL. Here I am, Your Excellency.

AUTONOM SYGIZMUNDOVICH. Seize him! Seize him! Tie him down!

PAVEL SERGEEVICH. Most respected comrades, this is our cook!

AUTONOM SYGIZMUNDOVICH. Shut up!

PAVEL SERGEEVICH. I swear to God, she is. She washes my socks and even heats up my meatballs. I swear to God!

OLYMP VALERIANOVICH. It's perfectly clear – he's quite mad.

NADEJDA PETROVNA. Dear gentlemen, may God hear my words: she did heat up his meatballs. Nastia, you slut, answer your mistress: did you or did you not heat up his meatballs?

NASTIA. Well, of course I did.

NADEJDA PETROVNA. Do you hear that, do you hear that, gentlemen? She's confessed, she's confessed.

OLYMP VALERIANOVICH. Your Imperial Highness . . .

NADEJDA PETROVNA. What 'Highness'? She's Nastia Poopkin. I even have her passport. Poopkin, Anastasia Nikolaevna Poopkin.

OLYMP VALERIANOVICH. What do you mean – Poopkin?

NADEJDA PETROVNA. I mean Poopkin, from Plopogrod.

OLYMP VALERIANOVICH. Your Imperial Highness! What does she mean – Poopkin?

NASTIA. That's my name, in point of fact.

VALERIAN OLYMPOVICH. Poopkin?

NASTIA. Poopkin.

OLYMP VALERIANOVICH. And your uncle?

NASTIA. What about my uncle?

OLYMP VALERIANOVICH. Do you have an uncle?

NASTIA. I certainly do.

OLYMP VALERIANOVICH. And is he a Grand Duke?

NASTIA. No. He's a mortuary attendant.

OLYMP VALERIANOVICH. Gentlemen, I'm starting to feel rather dizzy.

ZARKHIN. It's all over! Everything is ruined.

NARKIS SMARAGDOVICH. The Renaissance has collapsed.

OLYMP VALERIANOVICH. So that's it. It's happened all over again. It's all vanished. Nothing exists – neither her, nor me, nor you.

PAVEL SERGEEVICH. Comrades, it's true that nothing exists. But my words will live for ever, my heroism is immortal, comrades. The fact I've called the heir to the Russian throne a silly cow, this cannot be erased from the escutcheon of history. Can you imagine the future that beckons me? Probably, for my Great Declaration, they'll let me in and out of the Kremlin without a security check. For my Great Declaration they will erect hospitals sacred to the name of Pavel Sergeevich Guliachkin. Perhaps, comrades, you probably imagined that when they took the grocery away from me and painted over the sign that I was ruined? Not a bit of it! Comrades, now I'll be able to put up a new sign and under it I'll sell the most expensive things that money can buy. I will! I'll sell everything, everything!

ILYINKIN. Comrade Guliachkin, forgive us. It's all his fault. He's responsible.

PAVEL SERGEEVICH. Well, my friends, so we're suddenly frightened, are we? You think you can turn my bottom into a kind of picture gallery and get away with it, do you? You think you can turn my identity upside down, and get away with it, eh? Nice try, friends, but you made a big mistake. This time it's curtains. I shall destroy you all! Each of you!

STEPAN STEPANOVICH. Spare us. Forgive us! We didn't do anything wrong!

PAVEL SERGEEVICH. Silence! Don't you know who I am? Don't you realise what I can do? When it comes to defending an idea, I'm capable of anything. They even turned me into a dowry for the sake of an idea. Now I'll marry Varvara to the whole of Russia. Varvara, stand here, choose anyone you like.

VOICES. Choose me! Here, choose me! No, choose me!

FELIZIATA GORDEEVNA. My husband, Varvara. Choose my husband!

TOSIA. Choose Papa!

SIUSIA. Yes, choose Papa!

ILYINKINA. My husband!

NADEJDA PETROVNA. Varvara dear, choose.

VARVARA SERGEEVNA. Well, he's got to be passionate and wear pince-nez.

PAVEL SERGEEVICH. Varvara!

OLYMP VALERIANOVICH. How can it have happened, gentlemen? I saw it myself, with my own eyes. Just here. Right on this spot. I saw our dear beloved Motherland, our true and authentic Mother Russia rise like a phoenix, out of the chest.

STEPAN STEPANOVICH. Out of which chest?

AUTONOM SYGIZMUNDOVICH. I knocked the lock off like this.

OLYMP VALERIANOVICH. And inside we found Russia.

They open the chest. Inside is IVAN IVANOVICH, *with the pot still on his head. He climbs out of the chest.*

IVAN IVANOVICH. I've heard every word. I know it all. Gentlemen, stay calm and freeze, since you're all going to be hanged. Militia! Militia!

OLYMP VALERIANOVICH. Forgive me, comrade, but what's it got to do with the Militia?

IVAN IVANOVICH. I shall report everything to them straight away.

OLYMP VALERIANOVICH. Report what?

IVAN IVANOVICH. That you, in your own flat, in this very room, have overthrown the Soviet regime.

NASTIA. Oh Vania, sweetheart, do stop going on!

OLYMP VALERIANOVICH. Maybe it seemed like that to you, comrade. But, I give you my word it isn't true. We have witnesses. Here, here is a Communist.

IVAN IVANOVICH. Where is there a Communist?

OLYMP VALERIANOVICH. Here, Pavel Sergeevich.

IVAN IVANOVICH. Pavel Sergeevich? For your information, citizens, Pavel Sergeevich is an imposter, a False Dimitry, and not a Communist.

PAVEL SERGEEVICH. Who's an imposter? Me, an imposter? Me? Comrades! I am the tribune of the working class. I even have calluses. Look, what huge calluses I have on my hands. But that's nothing to the calluses on my feet – they defy belief.

IVAN IVANOVICH. Prove it.

PAVEL SERGEEVICH. I will prove it.

IVAN IVANOVICH. How?

PAVEL SERGEEVICH. Call the Foreign Minister here and just ask *him* if I'm a Communist or not, comrades.

AUTONOM SYGIZMUNDOVICH. You're on to a loser, comrade, he's even got a mandate.

IVAN IVANOVICH. Where is the mandate?

AUTONOM SYGIZMUNDOVICH (*taking it out of the briefcase*). Here.

IVAN IVANOVICH (*seizes the paper*). Now I've got you, citizens.

PAVEL SERGEEVICH. Hold him, hold him! Where are you going? Where are you going?

IVAN IVANOVICH. To the Militia, citizens, to the Militia!

IVAN IVANOVICH *runs off.*

PAVEL SERGEEVICH. Save us! Save us!

EVERYONE. Save us! Save us!

PAVEL SERGEEVICH. I'm done for! I'm done for! They'll hang me!

OLYMP VALERIANOVICH. What do you mean, they'll hang you? Who would dare hang you, comrade?

NADEJDA PETROVNA. Pavel dear, what's the matter with you?

PAVEL SERGEEVICH. Everybody, fellow God-fearing Christians, the thing is, actually, I wrote out the mandate myself.

VARVARA SERGEEVNA. Please say goodbye to Mummy for me, I think I'm going to die.

OLYMP VALERIANOVICH. You wrote it out yourself? What do you mean? But you *are* still a member of the Party, aren't you?

PAVEL SERGEEVICH. No, comrades. I'm not really . . .

OLYMP VALERIANOVICH. Not really what?

PAVEL SERGEEVICH. Comrades, I'm not really anybody, really.

OLYMP VALERIANOVICH. That's it! It's all over. It's all ruined. Everyone's a fake. She's a fake, he's a fake, maybe even we're fakes as well?

AUTONOM SYGIZMUNDOVICH. Never mind, people, nowadays even mandates are fake.

ARIADNA PAVLINOVNA. Comrades, I can't possibly be arrested, I have children, see, here they are, Tosia and Siusia, my dear little ones.

STEPAN STEPANOVICH. Citizen, we are all little ones.

PAVEL SERGEEVICH. Mummy, tell them I'm a fool, tell them that I'm stupid. Maybe they don't hang the educationally challenged.

NADEJDA PETROVNA. They'd never believe it of you, Pavel dear, they'd never believe it.

PAVEL SERGEEVICH. They would believe it, Mummy, I'm sure they would.

EVERYONE. They're coming! We're done for! It's the end! Who's that? What? What?

Enter IVAN IVANOVICH, *who sits on the chair and cries.*

OLYMP VALERIANOVICH. What? What?

IVAN IVANOVICH. They said they wouldn't.

OLYMP VALERIANOVICH. Wouldn't what?

IVAN IVANOVICH. Wouldn't arrest you.

A pause.

PAVEL SERGEEVICH. God Almighty, if they won't even arrest us, how can we live, Mummy? How can we live?

The End.